2824 JVD FG
(158)

B27507

One in five

Special needs in education

SERIES EDITOR
Ron Gulliford, Professor of Education,
University of Birmingham

One in five

The assessment and incidence of special educational needs

Paul Croll and **Diana Moses**

Routledge & Kegan Paul
London, Boston and Henley.

First published in 1985
by Routledge & Kegan Paul plc
14 Leicester Square, London WC2H 7PH, England
9 Park Street, Boston, Mass. 02108, USA and
Broadway House, Newtown Road,
Henley-on-Thames, Oxon RG9 1EN, England

Set in Baskerville
and printed and bound in Great Britain
by Butler and Tanner Ltd.,
Frome, Somerset.

Library of Congress Cataloging in Publication Data

Croll, Paul.
One in five.
Bibliography: p.
Includes index.
1. Handicapped children – Education – England – Leicester
(Leicestershire)   2. Handicapped children – Rating of –
England – Leicester (Leicestershire)   3. Mainstreaming in
education – England – Leicester (Leicestershire)   I. Moses,
Diana.   II. Title.
LC4036.G6C76   1985   371.9'0942542   84–29838

British Library CIP data also available

ISBN 0-7102-0322-5

Contents

	Foreword *by Professor Gerald Bernbaum*	vii
	Acknowledgments	xiv
1	Introduction	1
2	Some background issues	11
3	The teacher's view of special educational needs in the junior classroom	21
4	Teachers' views on the aetiology of special educational needs	42
5	Attitudes towards integration	50
6	Reading achievement and teacher assessment	60
7	Testing and assessment in junior classrooms	76
8	Provision	92
9	Pupils and teachers in the classroom	118
10	Other aspects of classroom behaviour and special educational needs	135
11	Summary and implications	147
Appendix	Research design, sampling and analysis	154
	Bibliography	164
	Index	167

Foreword

This study has its origins in the publication of the *Report of the Committee of Inquiry into the Education of Handicapped Children and Young People*. The Report, better known as the Warnock Report after the name of the Chairman of the Committee of Inquiry, Dame Mary Warnock, appeared in 1978 and, in its broad recommendations, reflected much of the educational thinking with respect to special educational needs which had been developed in the previous twenty years. Central to the recommendations of the Warnock Report was the view that the concept of special educational needs should be broadened to encompass a wider range of pupils and young people with learning difficulties. By this change of definition the Report estimated that, at various times, as many as one in five pupils in ordinary schools might fall into one of the categories of special educational needs.

On reading the Report I was immediately aware of certain problematic aspects of its recommendations. It seemed to me that the ordinary classroom teacher would become a central agent in the determination of which children fall into the category of special educational needs and that, moreover, the judgments of the teachers were likely to be influenced both by their own training experience and by the educational contexts in which they worked. It was also possible to argue that there might be variation in the extent to which teachers were prepared to define children as having special educational needs, depending upon the availability of local remedial services.

Shortly after the publication of the Report, therefore, I approached the Department of Education and Science and, with the assistance of officials from the Department and members of the Inspectorate, developed some of my ideas in more detail. As a result of those discussions, the DES issued a small grant of just under £5,000 for a pilot study. Diana Moses was appointed as the Research Assistant on the project and the report that she produced suggested clearly that the ordinary classroom teacher was indeed central to the definition of children with special educational needs, and that such ordinary teachers did face a variety of difficulties in making their assessments. Teachers, it appeared, found it difficult to differentiate between the slow learner and the child with specific reading problems. Ability and achievement seemed to be defined very much in terms of reading skills whilst other skills were, relatively speaking, overlooked. The pilot study suggested that teachers had difficulty in evaluating the opinions of other teachers as expressed on record cards and that they were not efficient in administering and analysing standardised tests of ability and attainment. Most teachers, it appeared from our pilot study, tended to prefer their own individual assessments of a child's potential based upon their own impressions of the pupil's class work, behaviour and attitude. The pilot study also showed that there was a great deal of sympathy amongst classroom teachers for the Warnock view that a much greater effort should be made to integrate children with special educational needs, of whatever kind, into normal classroom work. It was also clear from the small-scale investigation that special needs were not exclusive to inner city schools, but were to be found across the whole range of junior schools.

All of these findings suggested that a larger-scale study would be rewarding and it was particularly encouraging that the Department of Education and Science followed up the pilot investigation with a large grant for a more detailed study on the assessment and incidence of special educational needs. The research team consisted of myself and Paul Croll as Co-Directors and, initially, Diana Moses and Jane Wright as Research Associates. Jane Wright left to take up a headship about halfway through the project and was, at a later date, replaced by Valerie Brooks. The bulk of the detailed research and analysis, therefore, was conducted by Paul Croll and Diana Moses, and it is appropriate that the major report of the study should appear under their joint names.

Like all research projects, however, the study was not without its difficulties. There were the usual problems of research design, sampling and reviewing the relevant literature but as we worked on the project we faced the unusual situation that the administrative and legislative framework was changing about us. The government and the local authorities were acting upon the recommendations of the Warnock Report throughout the early years of the 1980s and thus the situation that existed with respect to practice and policy at the end of the study was different from that pertaining when our work began. Paul Croll and Diana Moses elaborate in the text some of the problems that were faced but the reader should keep in mind that the current situation with respect to the policy for the education of children with special educational needs is different from that described in the early section of the study, though these legal and administrative changes do not affect the significance of the findings described here, which relate to the practices of classroom teachers. The most important change has been that the old ten statutory categories of handicap have, as a result of legislation in 1981, been replaced with the broader concept of special educational needs. The Warnock Report argued that to classify children in terms of the nature of their handicaps was inadequate, and could be misleading. Many handicapped children suffer from multiple disadvantage but their major handicap, defined from a medical standpoint, might not be that which is the most significant with respect to their educational problems and progress. The newer perspectives highlighted by Warnock focus attention on the child's educational needs rather than on the disabilities from which he or she might suffer.

Equally fundamental to the Warnock Report's recommendations was the view that the concept of special educational needs should apply to a very much larger proportion of the school population than had previously been regarded as in need of special education. The Warnock Report argued that special educational needs should be regarded as a continuum which might extend from the pupils who were in special schools through to a substantial number of children in ordinary schools and classrooms who had educational difficulties that might require some form of special treatment. The view of the Committee was that about one in six children at any time and up to one in five at some time during their school career might require special educational provision. This broadening of the concept of special educational needs, which has now been accepted, inevitably involved ordinary classroom teachers becoming more intimately concerned with children with special educational needs than had previously been the case.

The study undertaken at Leicester and reported here by Paul Croll and Diana Moses addressed itself to some of the problems arising from the new role given to classroom teachers with respect to the identification of children with special educational needs. The study was conducted in two main parts. First there was a survey of 428 junior-class teachers in 61 schools selected at random in 10 local education authorities spread across the country. The teachers were all interviewed at length and invited to discuss how they dealt with the assessment of special educational needs, their testing and record-keeping activities, their contacts with outside specialist agencies such as the School Psychological Service. The teachers were also asked about their experience of and attitudes to the integration of handi-capped children in ordinary classrooms. Alongside these interviews with class teachers interviews were also carried out with head teachers and remedial teachers in the same schools. Second, a detailed study was made of thirty-four second-year junior classes with children between the ages of eight and nine. From these classes of children information was gathered from the teachers about the special educational needs of the pupils and, in addition, the children were given tests of reading and of non-verbal reasoning. Following this initial stage a sample of children identified as having special educational needs and a control sample of other children were selected for systematic observation. Thus it became possible to consider teacher assessment of pupils alongside the performance and behaviour of pupils. In these ways consideration could be given both to the central role of the classroom teacher and to the part that the teacher's perspectives might play in determining and influencing definitions of special educational needs. It was possible, therefore, to examine the pattern of special educational needs based upon teacher assessment and to consider the factors which might determine that pattern. The study, therefore, explores the characteristics of the children being assessed and the characteristics of the institutional setting of school and local authority in which the teacher worked.

It should be clear from the description of the study that we gathered a great deal of information about schools, teachers, pupils and local authority provision for special educational needs. Indeed, the data reported here are of such detail that, leaving aside any particular interest in special educational needs, the material is a remarkable contribution to the study of schools and the educational process. The main conclusions of the investigation should provide encouragement not only to the authors of the Warnock Report but also to teachers in ordinary classrooms who emerge with credit for facing difficult tasks under circumstances which are not always favourable to them. The authors of the report, Paul Croll and Diana Moses, provide a detailed summary of their results at various points in the volume and it is not appropriate for me to repeat our findings in detail. Briefly, however, the study reveals that the incidence of special educational needs in junior classrooms, as estimated by the classroom teachers in junior schools, is very close to the estimate contained in the Warnock Report that between one in five and one in six children have special educational needs. Teachers recognise also that children so identified are, for the most part, the responsibility of the ordinary school. What is particularly interesting, however, is the way in which pupils' learning difficulties dominate the criteria employed by teachers and that within those criteria the most commonly identified specific learning difficulty was the problem with reading. After learning problems, behaviour problems form the next largest category of special educational needs as viewed by the teachers. Children with behaviour difficulties often had learning problems also, but the teachers were able to distinguish the variety of behavioural difficulties and, moreover, to separate a child who had behaviour problems from those who necessarily presented discipline difficulties within the class. The study shows also that all schools have pupils with special educational needs. It was not the case that there were intense concentrations of such children in a few difficult schools.

Overall the teachers seem sensitively aware of the difficulties experienced by a sizeable minority of their pupils. The teachers, moreover, believe that the great majority of children with difficulties, including those with physical handicaps, should be taught in an ordinary school. In fact, the teachers were more enthusiastic about the integration into ordinary classrooms of children with physical or sensory handicaps than they were for those with severe learning problems or behavioural difficulties. It was a further encouraging sign that where a teacher had had experience of integrating a child with a particular handicap in the regular classroom then that teacher was more likely to have a positive attitude towards future integration.

The study does, however, also reveal certain problems faced by the teachers with respect to the formal and informal assessment techniques available to them. Most teachers use standardised tests in some form or other when making the assessment of their pupils. Given the emphasis upon reading it was not surprising to find a standardised test of reading was the most common form of assessment employed. Unfortunately, as other recent work has suggested, the tests were rarely used well and were not really adequate for the identification of learning difficulties. Further problems arose through the administration of the tests and the keeping of records which was not well done in many schools. There is no doubt that the teachers have an ambivalence towards standardised tests; on the one hand perceiving the tests as being devised by experts with authority and thus conveying apparently objective information about pupils, but, on the other hand, finding themselves anxious about their own lack of professional training in the whole business of testing and therefore somewhat confused about precisely what kind of abilities the tests test and, hence, their overall value.

Amongst the unique features of the work that we undertook was the use of systematic observation to describe the classroom experiences of children with special educational needs and to describe some of the difficulties which they pose for teachers. Such children appear to have a distinctive pattern of classroom behaviour characterised in the main by relatively low levels of engagement with work in hand. Although the teachers spend about twice as much time working individually with these children as they do with other pupils, that time necessarily remains a small proportion of their total time in class. The study suggests strongly that the level of work engagement of children with special needs was particularly influenced by the context of their activities. It seems, for example, that where the teacher works with a small group of children, the outcome for those with special educational needs is notably encouraging.

I believe, therefore, that the whole study offers a valuable insight into the workings of schools and classrooms and, most particularly of course, into the ways in which teachers relate to pupils with special educational needs. The study is encouraging with respect to the consensual elements in the teachers' judgments and in the way those judgments seem to reflect the analysis of the Warnock Report. It is encouraging also to note the broad sympathy that teachers have for the integration of children with special educational needs, most especially where those needs might arise from physical or sensory handicap. What is less encouraging, however, and might require further consideration by teachers and policy makers, is the uncertainty that clearly exists in the relationship between the schools and the teachers on the one hand, and the specialist advisory services on the other. A similar concern could be expressed about the inadequate testing that goes on in many schools where the tests are not entirely appropriate, frequently out of date, and sometimes misunderstood. It might be reasonably hoped that if testing is to remain an extensive feature of junior schools then the teachers, in their initial teacher education and in their in-service work, should be better prepared for the tasks. Finally, the emphasis upon reading in junior schools and the testing of reading is clearly a matter that requires further reflection. Close association between poor reading performance on the part of pupils and their later definition as having special education needs has been established by this study. A dramatic reduction in the numbers defined as having special educational needs could be achieved either by de-emphasising the significance of reading in the judgments made about pupils, or, it might be suggested, by a determined effort to improve the teaching of reading to young children in schools. The former seems, justly, to be both unlikely and unacceptable, whilst the latter approach might provide a reasonable basis for development in the teaching of young children over the next ten years.

I believe that the study reported here provides data which are both important and useful in the discussion of future policy with respect to special educational needs and, as the originator of the project, I wish to thank all who have worked on it over the three-year period and, most particularly, those in the schools that have worked with us. Needless to say, the final product is the responsibility of the research team; neither the teachers who helped us nor the DES have responsibility for the views expressed in this book.

Gerald Bernbaum

Acknowledgments

The research reported here was carried out at the School of Education, University of Leicester, and was funded by a grant from the Department of Education and Science. The Project was directed by Professor Gerald Bernbaum and Paul Croll, and the full-time research staff were Paul Croll, Diana Moses and (for the first two years of the project) Jane Wright. The authors are grateful to Professor Bernbaum for his support and advice and for his detailed comments on the draft text, and to Mrs Wright for the substantial contributions she made to the planning of the work and to the collection of data. We are also grateful to Mrs Barbara Hughes, who was project secretary for most of the period in which research was being conducted and whose organisational skills greatly eased the complex process of data collection.

The research team had the benefit of a DES Steering Committee, and we should particularly like to thank Miss M. d'Armenia, who was chairman of the committee for most of the period of the research, Mr E. Basire, the committee secretary, Mr F. Green, HMI, Mr C. Marshall, HMI, Professor M. Clark, and Professor M. Chazan, for their valuable advice.

The research was conducted in ten local education authorities, and we should like to thank the various education officers, advisers and educational psychologists who helped arrange data collection and otherwise facilitated the research. Most of all, we thank the 500 heads and teachers in 61 primary schools who made time available to talk to us, and the 34 teachers who allowed us to spend time in their classrooms. The interest they showed in the research, their enthusiasm for talking about their pupils and their concern for their difficulties made data collection an enjoyable and rewarding experience.

1 Introduction

The Warnock Report

The publication of the Warnock Report in 1978 was a major landmark in the development of thinking about special education in Britain. The ideas and recommendations contained in the Report have informed all subsequent debate in the area and are fundamental to the research reported here. Through the incorporation of many of the Warnock recommendations in the 1981 Education Act they have also influenced the statutory framework within which the education system operates. The content of the Report is best seen as part of a development of current thinking rather than a new departure in the field of special education. It incorporates much of current thinking in the area, and many of the suggestions in the Report embody the best of current practice. What is new in the Warnock Report, however, is the way that special education is extended in scope and is made of central concern to the educational system generally. It is seen as something relevant to all schools and all teachers, rather than as a separate part of the system and the concern of a limited number of specialists. This wider concept of special education provides the context of the research reported here.

The title of the Committee, 'Committee of Enquiry into the Education of Handicapped Children and Young People', derives from the traditional notion of special education as involving a small, distinct and relatively easily identifiable group of handicapped children. These were children who fell into one of the ten statutory categories of handicap; blind pupils, partially sighted pupils, deaf pupils, partially hearing pupils, educationally subnormal pupils, epileptic pupils, maladjusted pupils, physically handicapped pupils, pupils suffering from a speech defect and delicate pupils (DES, 1978, p.380). At the time of the publication of the Warnock Report, 1.8 per

1

cent of the school population was in one of these categories, educated, for the most part, in special schools. By far the largest group consisted of pupils classified as educationally subnormal. This category was further divided into educationally subnormal (severe) and educationally subnormal (moderate), most children falling into the moderate, ESN(M) category. The next largest category of handicap was that of maladjusted pupils.

Children placed in one of these categories have usually been educated at an appropriate special school. In the case of children with very severe handicaps, this special school placement is likely to have resulted from their early contact with medical services, but for most children the referral for special education is likely to have arisen from their experience at school. Particularly in the case of children classified as educationally subnormal (moderate) and those classified as maladjusted, special schooling has normally been preceded by a period in mainstream schooling followed by referral for special education, usually at the initiative of the head teacher. This procedure, which, following the 1981 Act, now includes a statement of the child's special educational needs, involves the school medical officer and, in particular, an educational psychologist.

The period leading up to the Warnock Report saw a growing movement in educational thinking towards bringing special education out of its isolation. In particular, there was an emphasis on the value and feasibility of educating handicapped children in ordinary schools alongside their non-handicapped peers. This process, known in Britain as 'integration', has been the focus of a recent research project conducted by the National Foundation for Educational Research which documents a number of instances of the integration of children from the old statutory categories into ordinary schools (Hegarty and Pocklington, 1981a, 1981b). This gradual inclusion of the handicapped in normal schooling is part of a general tendency within western educational systems. Perhaps the best known and most influential example is Public Law 94–142, which eventuated in integration programmes (known as 'mainstreaming') in the United States. A number of examples of the integration of the handicapped in Europe are given by Hegarty and Pocklington (1981a, pp. 20–30). The Warnock Report supports this move towards integration while recognising the difficulties involved and the improvement in special educational provision in ordinary schools which will be necessary. Further integration is seen in the Report as a long-term development for which careful planning will be necessary.

There is, however, a substantial change proposed in the Report and now incorporated into the 1981 legislation with regard to this small group of handicapped children, namely the proposal to abolish the ten statutory categories of handicap and replace them with the notion of 'special educational needs'. The Report argues that to classify children in terms of the nature of their handicaps is inadequate and sometimes misleading, partly because many handicapped children have more than one handicap, and that which is the major handicap from a medical point of view may not be that which is most relevant to their educational problems. Additionally, however, the new terminology focuses attention on the child's educational needs rather than on the disabilities from which he or she suffers. The Report suggests that in future handicapped children should be assessed in terms of the special educational provision they require, rather than categorised according to the nature of their handicaps. These recommendations were included in the 1981 Education Act and in the circular of guidance to local education authorities which followed it.

Even more fundamental, however, was the proposal in the Report that the concept of special educational needs should apply to a very much larger proportion of the school population than had previously been regarded as in need of special education. The Report argued that there was not a distinct group of children with special educational needs corresponding approximately to the children in the old categories of handicap, but that special educational needs should be regarded as a continuum which should extend from pupils currently in special schools to include a substantial number of children in ordinary schools who had educational difficulties requiring some form of special treatment. For example, the Committee proposed that the old statutory category, 'educationally subnormal', in which about two-thirds of children in special education are placed, should be replaced by the term 'children with learning difficulties', and that this term should be used 'to describe both those children who are currently categorised as educationally subnormal and those with educational difficulties who are often at present the concern of remedial services' (DES, 1978, p.43).

Basing its estimate on various epidemiological studies of children's difficulties, principally the research conducted in the Isle of Wight (Rutter, Tizard and Whitmore, 1970) and the research conducted by the National Children's Bureau (Pringle, Butler and Davie, 1966), the Report concluded:

> The planning of services for children and young people should be based on the assumption that about one in six children at any time and up to one in five children at some time during their school career will require some form of special educational provision.

Special needs and the ordinary school

The introduction of this 'broad concept' of special educational needs has considerable implications for the educational system and for all schools and teachers. It helps to break down the barriers between special and mainstream education by its double emphasis, on not only the kind of educational provision necessary for handicapped children but also the need experienced by a great many children for special educational help of some kind. The 'broad concept' insists that a concern with special educational needs should be a central feature of the educational system, a point which, as the Report clearly recognises, has considerable implications for teachers in ordinary schools:

> This [the broad concept of special needs] means that a teacher of a mixed ability class of thirty children even in an ordinary school should be aware that possibly as many as six of them may require some form of special educational provision at some time during their school life and about four or five of them may require special educational provision at any given time (p. 41).

The notion of special needs contained in the Warnock Report rests on an educational judgment about the sort of provision which particular children require and the extent to which the 'specialness' of the provision made for a particular child goes beyond the variation in approach which will occur between any two children. These are judgments which will be made for the most part by ordinary teachers in ordinary classrooms. Whether children are subsequently referred for special help outside the school, receive additional help in the school or stay in the classroom for their needs to be met by the regular teacher, class teachers will be responsible for making the initial assessment. The obligation on the class teacher to perceive and initiate

4

remedial treatment of learning difficulties at an early stage was emphasised by the Warnock Committee:

> Since the large majority of children who are likely to require special educational provision will manifest their difficulties for the first time in school, they will have to be identified. Close and continuous observation of all children by their teachers is therefore essential and for this to be effective teachers must be equipped to notice signs of special need. Moreover, having noticed such signs in a child they must appreciate the importance of early assessment of these needs and must know when and where to refer for special help.

The problem, however, is not simply one of equipping teachers to notice the signs of special need but in deciding of what such signs actually consist. Teachers have not been given a clear functional description of what constitutes special need against which they can assess particular children. Consequently, such judgments are likely to be made by teachers in a variety of ways and are likely to be influenced not only by levels of performance and types of behaviour of individual children but also by such factors as the child's relative standing among his classmates, the teacher's own expectations, knowledge and attitudes with regard to special needs, and institutional factors such as school and local authority policy and provision in this area.

The extent of provision for special educational needs is obviously crucially important. The Warnock Committee defines children as having special needs if it is necessary that special provision should be made for them, and this definition is also included in the 1981 Education Act: 'For the purposes of this Act a child has special educational needs if he has a learning difficulty which calls for special educational provision to be made for him.' Special educational provision for a child is defined in the Act as 'educational provision which is additional to, or otherwise different from, the educational provision made generally for children of his age in schools maintained by the local education authority concerned'. It is, however, far from clear that the relationship between needs and provision is as straightforward as this suggests. A direct relationship between needs and provision would imply that needs are absolute and that provision could be evaluated in terms of how adequately it met them. It seems more likely that there is an inter-relationship between the needs and provision in the area of special education, particularly when the notion of special education is extended to the point where it applies to perhaps a fifth of the school-age population. Assessment of the needs of these children will probably be influenced by the nature and extent of provision available. Consequently, it is necessary to see provision not only as a response to teacher assessments but as one of the factors which may influence them.

The 'broad concept' of special educational needs contained in the Warnock Report and the explicit responsibilities placed on schools and local authorities by the legislation which followed the Report imply a new way of looking at problems which have always been the concern of the mainstream of the school system. The difficulties experienced by a substantial minority of pupils have not changed following the Warnock Report, and schools have always had a responsibility to offer appropriate education to all their pupils. It may also be that in many cases the ways in which schools defined and met the difficulties of their pupils already involved the principles contained in the Warnock Report and the 1981 Act, and that what is needed is an extension of the best practice rather than an entirely new approach.

Although, as has been suggested above, the 'newness' of the Warnock approach should not be over-emphasised, there is no doubt that the approach does present teachers, schools and others concerned in education with difficulties of both a practical and logical kind. There is evidence that this is an area of their work in which teachers do not feel themselves well equipped by their training. In a recent survey of primary teachers in Nottinghamshire, Bassey found that 60 per cent thought their training had been 'inadequate' in helping them to deal with slow learners and only 13 per cent thought it had been 'good'. Of twenty-two areas of primary education, only in the area of teaching gifted children was the training rated as less satisfactory than in that of teaching slow learners. The area in which the next highest level of dissatisfaction occurred was the teaching of reading: here 50 per cent thought their training had been 'inadequate' (Bassey, 1981). Of the teachers interviewed in the present study, 60 per cent said they had received no special training in the teaching of reading, even during their initial training, and 80 per cent said they had received no special training in the area of special educational needs. The difficulties which teachers can experience in this area are illustrated by a study of an in-service programme on special educational needs conducted as part of the present research. When presented with a checklist relating to children's skills, teachers initially thought that they could complete it rapidly for certain children in their class. They later reported, however, that they did not know the children's strengths and weaknesses as well as they had thought and that they had had to devise procedures for learning about them (Brooks, 1983).

The present research

The research reported here addresses itself to two major themes: the extension of the concept of special educational needs to include up to a fifth of the school population, and the central role of the ordinary class teacher in this process. More specifically, the project was particularly concerned with the ways in which junior-school teachers assess pupils in their classes as having special educational needs, and the incidence of special educational needs consequent upon these assessments.

The restriction of the research to the junior age range (in Britain, children aged seven to eleven) was partly a question of the availability of resources but also arises from the particular importance of the relationship between the teacher and her class in the primary school, where a child is normally taught for a year by a single teacher. The problems associated with initial assessments of children when they come into the infant school are beyond the scope of the present study.

A full description of the research procedures is given in the Appendix, but a brief account will also be presented here. The study can be divided into two main aspects, a survey of teachers and a study of children. For the survey of teachers, personal interviews were carried out with a sample of 428 junior-class teachers in 61 schools selected at random in 10 local education authorities across the country. These interviews lasted about an hour and dealt with the teachers' assessments of the special educational needs of pupils in the classes, testing and record-keeping procedures they used, contact with outside specialist agencies such as the School Psychological Service and experience of, and attitudes to, the integration of handicapped children in the ordinary classroom. Interviews were also carried out with the head teachers and remedial teachers in these schools.

The study of children concentrated on thirty-four second-year junior classes (children aged eight to nine). In these classes, information was gathered from the teacher about the special educational needs of the pupils, and tests of reading and of non-verbal reasoning were carried out. Following this, a sample of children identified as having special educational needs and a control sample of other children were selected for systematic observation. An observer, a member of the research team, spent about two weeks in each classroom using an observation system to record children's activities and interactions at ten-second intervals. This part of the research made it possible to relate teacher assessments of pupils to aspects of their performance and behaviour.

The approach to special educational needs adopted in the research and carried out in the manner outlined above was designed to explore two aims: first, the central role of the classroom teacher in assessing and meeting special educational needs, and, second, the influence upon our view of special educational needs that is exerted by the teacher's approach to the task. Having established a pattern of special educational needs based on teacher assessment, the research then considers factors which underlie these assessments. These include characteristics of the children being assessed, but may also involve characteristics of the teacher and of institutional factors related to the school and local authority.

The chapters which follow begin with an analysis of special educational needs as identified by the teachers and then move on to consider other sorts of information about children and their difficulties. Chapter 2 gives a brief look at some background issues. Chapter 3 deals with the assessments teachers make of the special educational needs of their pupils. This chapter is central to the research project as it shows the incidence of various kinds of special needs as they emerge from teacher assessments, which can be compared with the incidence of special needs assumed in the Warnock Report. The two subsequent chapters will deal with teachers' views: Chapter 4 considers teachers' views on the causes of children's difficulties, and Chapter 5 looks at teacher attitudes towards the integration of handicapped children in the regular classroom. Later chapters go beyond teacher views and teacher assessments and look at other characteristics of pupils and of schools and classrooms. Chapter 6 relates the teachers' assessments to pupil scores on reading tests and to other pupil characteristics. Chapter 7 details the extent of testing procedures of various kinds in junior classrooms, and Chapter 8 deals with the extent and organisation of provision for children with special educational needs. Chapters 9 and 10 describe the classroom activities and interactions of children with special educational needs compared with those of other children in the class. Finally, Chapter 11 summarises the results and their implications, and there is an Appendix containing details of the research design and data-gathering procedures.

Any research project faces something of a problem in trying to discuss issues of general educational relevance from research conducted at a particular point in time, and this problem is particularly acute in the case of the present research. The data collection was conducted after the publication of the Warnock Report, while the 1981 Education Act was before Parliament but before the circular of guidance to local authorities on the implementation of the Act was issued. As a result we have problems of terminology. For instance, discussions with teachers about integration were formulated in terms of the then-prevailing categories of handicap, which are therefore key terms in Chapter 5. Elsewhere in this work the categories are little used. In the between-two-worlds period of data collection, the research was conducted in a changing situation and one which may have changed further since the completion of the project. The awkwardness of the circumstance will be seen particularly in the discussion of provision in Chapter 8, where the situation described was that existing before LEAs had had the new responsibilities placed on them.

To admit this awkwardness is not, however, to discount the validity of the results: the attitudes, assessments, procedures and provisions analysed here, which underlie the thinking that led to the Education Act of 1981 and its implementation, will continue to exert a considerable influence on the way in which special educational needs are identified and met. In particular, as is argued in Chapter 2, the way in which classroom teachers view special educational needs and the degree of congruence between their view and the view embodied in legislation is fundamental to the success of the new procedures. When the research was conducted, LEA officers were very much aware of the Warnock Report and its implications but this awareness was not general in schools. As will be shown in Chapter 3, the extent to which teachers' views duplicated the assumptions of the Warnock Report could not be attributed to knowledge of the Report. The assessments teachers make of their pupils and which are reported here are influenced by a large number of factors of which the changing statutory context is only one. These assessments are, however, of vital importance in the area of special educational needs.

Most of the analyses reported in the subsequent chapters are based on an essential exploratory approach to the data in which it is not appropriate to report levels of statistical significance. This is because if the data are examined in a preliminary fashion to identify patterns and relationships then a level of statistical significance cannot be meaningfully calculated. However, in the case of the data on classroom behaviour reported in Chapter 9 and 10, explicit hypotheses were generated and these results are reported in terms of significance levels. In all these tables, results are described as statistically significant when the probability of their having occurred by chance, if the null hypothesis is true, is less than one in twenty ($p < .05$).

2   Some background issues

Problems of definition

The extension of the concept of special educational need to embrace large numbers of children whose educational needs can be met within the ordinary school raises in a particularly acute form the problems of definition which have always applied in the area of special education. The difficulties of logically distinguishing a group of pupils whose educational needs are 'special' from other children who nevertheless have needs particular to themselves which could be described as special, contrasted with the commonsense observation that some children do have difficulties and needs very different from those of the majority, have been recently summarised by D. N. Aspin (1982):

> In a sense, special education is tautologous: in so far as we are dealing with children and intend to bring about increases in their perception and understanding of the world and ability to come to terms with it, there is no difference in kind between one sort of interpersonal transaction devoted to educational ends, and another. Yet, in so far as certain children do seem to need an extraordinary degree of care and attention, in order to counteract the particular difficulties under which they labour, we *can* term such extra effort 'special', as being greater in degree, though not in kind from what 'normal' children require.

Aspin points out that such assessments are 'irreducibly evaluative' and that:

> Our use and understanding of concepts of special education is transactional and conventional in character because these in their turn are functions of the theoretical preconceptions of their practitioners. We approach problems in the field by a process of

11

negotiation and in terms of our interpersonal agreement that
serve to 'define the situation'.

Clearly, before we can profitably use the concept of special educational
need we have to be sure that there is a working agreement between
people concerned with education about what such needs are and the
sorts of children who have them.

To a certain extent the problem of definition applied to the children
(something under one in fifty) who were in the old statutory categories.
It has always been clear that there were children in special schools
whose difficulties were no more severe than those of other pupils who
had remained in ordinary schools, or, put the other way round, there
were children in ordinary schools whose difficulties were at least as
great as some special school children. Figures for the proportions
of children in various sorts of special provision in different local
education authorities, quoted in the Warnock Report, make it clear
that some of the variations between authorities reflect factors other
than the level of difficulty experienced by children. All this suggests
some variation, among teachers and others, in the practical definitions
of what constitutes special educational needs in the pre-Warnock
sense.

Such variation in practical definitions is, at least potentially, more
likely when the Warnock concept of special educational needs is
applied. The very much larger number of children involved, the
variation in existing arrangements for dealing with their special
difficulties and the lack of any clear functional definition of what
constitutes special needs, all suggest that there may be some difficulty
in arriving at the kind of interpersonal agreement about what
constitutes special needs described by Aspin.

The first major area of investigation of the research reported here is
into the views held by classroom teachers of special educational needs
in the ordinary school, the purpose being to study the way in which
this concept is applied by them to pupils in their classes in order to see
if the working definitions or commonsense assumptions about special
needs which are held by teachers match the estimates of such needs
contained in the Warnock Report. Given the central role of the class
teacher in assessment and identification it is important to consider
whether the notion of special educational need as set out in the
Warnock Report has any relation to the actual assessment, explicit or
implied, made by teachers in schools. Faced with the argument that

'every child is special' and with the *de facto* separation of about one child in fifty from the rest for attendance at a special school or class, teachers need to achieve a working agreement as to what constitutes special needs if they are to be able to play the major role assigned to them by the Warnock Committee.

Clearly the assessments made by teachers are crucial, both with regard to identifying individual children and in determining the incidence of special needs in the ordinary school. Indeed, it is not unreasonable to suggest that the epidemiology of special educational need, as defined by the Warnock Committee, is intimately linked with the question of definition of that need and to the processes and procedures for assessment. As has been argued above, if the concept of special need is to be meaningful to educationalists it will have to be based on agreement between practitioners rather than on arbitrarily defined criteria.

Some problems of assessment

It has often been pointed out that the criteria on which various estimates of children with learning difficulties are based involve norm-referenced tests or assessment procedures. Such procedures measure children's achievements by reference to the achievements of other children. For example, in the major British epidemiological study of children's difficulties (conducted on the Isle of Wight) which is one of the main sources of the Warnock estimates of incidence (Rutter *et al.*, 1970), children are described as being backward readers if they are twenty-eight months behind the average reading achievement of children of their age. This means that, whatever the overall level of achievement, some children must always be rated as the poorest achievers. Consequently, the notion of learning difficulties can be seen as being in a sense a statistical creation. The nature of the tests and their standardisation procedures necessarily involve a certain proportion of children appearing in the lowest ranking, whatever the nature of their achievements and educational need. In a test standardised to follow a normal curve, a known percentage of the children taking it must be one and two standard deviations above and below the mean. This definition of learning difficulties in terms of the achievements of other children also appears in the 1981 Education Act, where the definition of a child with learning difficulties includes

13

the statement: 'he has a significantly greater difficulty in learning than the majority of children of his age'.

It is worth noting that the problem of relative judgments appears to be an inevitable feature of the way in which we view children's educational performance rather than to be, as is sometimes suggested, a consequence of particular testing procedures or even of ideologically motivated demands that children be neatly sorted into groups or rank orders. It is sometimes suggested that criterion-referenced testing procedures provide a real alternative to norm-referencing and can present children's achievements in relation to an absolute standard of performance or to pre-set educational objectives. Criterion-referenced tests are designed not to discriminate among the population being tested so that there is considerable variation between the scores of individuals who can then be compared with one another, but to measure whether or not individuals have met a particular criterion. The most commonly given example of criterion-referenced tests is a driving test, which is concerned with whether or not individuals are competent drivers rather than whether they are average drivers or in the top 10 per cent of drivers and so on. In the context of school performance, criterion-referenced testing is concerned with similar yes/no operations.

Unfortunately, for most educational purposes it is difficult to see how we can escape the necessity to judge performance in comparison with other pupils. This seems particularly true in the area of learning difficulties but, it can be argued, it also applies in the area of any skills and abilities which have a developmental component. Put simply, if we are concerned to assess children, particularly children whose progress is giving cause for concern, any criterion, the skill or ability we decide a child does or does not have, is only meaningful against a concept of what is appropriate for a child at that age or developmental stage or with that level of educational opportunity. It is not simply that we do not have an absolute notion of the appropriate level of language development or reading competence that a five-year-old child should have, but that it is impossible to arrive at such a notion.

The reason that it is a matter for concern that a child entering junior school has no reading skills at all is that the great majority of children of that age and with two or more years' school experience do have particular levels of reading skills. If children did not start school until they were seven, then our notions of the appropriate performance for a seven-year-old would be different, while the sorts of performance

14

that give concern to teachers of ten-year-old pupils would not concern the teachers of seven-year-olds. If we were content not to assess academic achievements such as literacy and numeracy until maturation and schooling are relatively complete, then it might be possible to set standards not with reference to what most people achieve but with reference to the functional demands of contemporary society. But, if we want to assess children early so that we can identify those with difficulties and give them appropriate help, then we are inevitably going to view these children with reference to the achievements of their peers. This is, of course, not the same as insisting that tests be constructed so that the scores will follow a normal distribution.

In many discussions of criterion-referenced testing the relevance of the achievement of others in setting the criterion is explicitly recognised. Satterly (1981), for instance, in discussing the problem of setting the appropriate level of mastery in criterion-referenced tests, writes: 'Thus only two states are assessed, mastery and non-mastery of the objective. Given that these objectives are quickly mastered in most children a criterion of 90% accuracy might well be reasonable' (p. 50). Again, in an article concerned with criterion-referenced screening procedures for use for LEA screening of children with learning difficulties, Marshall and Wolfendale (1977) write:

> The rationale for including any item was that it should have a
> failure rate of between 6% and 15% of a normal school
> population of six and a half to seven and a half year olds.

and:

> a test which is criterion-referenced (i.e. referring to a fixed
> standard of achievement, in this case the level at which at least
> 85% of the population will be successful) is more appropriate for
> mass screening purposes than a norm-referenced measure (which
> has a wide spread of item difficulty and grades all children from
> the least to the most successful).

Thus, the advantage of Marshall and Wolfendale's procedures over many screening instruments is that it is particularly sensitive at the area of the distribution where children with learning difficulties are likely to score, but it cannot be regarded as a quite different kind of assessment procedure. To set a criterion in terms of what a fixed proportion of the population can achieve involves judging children with reference to others just as much as does a test designed to follow a

15

normal distribution. In fact it seems inevitable that any assessment procedure which can usefully identify children with learning difficulties will have a norm-referenced element, although that may not always be as explicit as in the case just quoted.

There is, however, another way of looking at the question of norm- and criterion-referenced testing. Just as the setting of a criterion involves a reference to what most children can be empirically expected to achieve, so norm-referenced testing inevitably involves a reference to the actual content of what we are trying to measure. The fact that a child is in the top 10 per cent on a test is usually of interest to educationalists only when they know what the content of the test is. Although judging children's performance by reference to other children inevitably condemns some to do well and some to do badly, it does not preclude us from looking at the actual content of these achievements in order to say whether or not we should be concerned if a child does badly. This point is taken up explicitly by the authors of the Isle of Wight study:

> Obviously whenever a test of intelligence or general attainment is given there must be some children whose scores are lower than those of other children just as some children will always be bottom of the class in reading or arithmetic. This will remain true however successfully children learn to read or perform on intelligence tests in future generations. If all children can read fluently the child who is worst in reading may not be handicapped at all. Thus, handicap must be judged in terms of what the child can and cannot do rather than in terms of his relative position in the class or on some test (Rutter *et al.*, 1970, pp. 348–51).

Consequently, in the Isle of Wight study the actual level of achievement for the children identified as having learning and other difficulties was examined. Examination confirmed the diagnosis of serious learning difficulties. The pupils identified as being the poorest achievers on norm-referenced tests were not victims of a test artefact but were children with very considerable difficulties:

> Put in these terms it is evident that the reading retarded children are indeed profoundly handicapped. They are, in fact, on a borderline of illiteracy. Furthermore their reading difficulties as shown by our follow-up studies are remarkably persistent so that

not only do they fail to benefit fully from their schooling but also many will be limited in the life they can lead after leaving school (*op cit*. p. 351).

As the Warnock Committee recognised, if children are to get the help they need they must be properly assessed, and, as the Isle of Wight research indicates, the children who come out poorest on assessment procedures have very genuine difficulties. However, it is less clear what the appropriate assessment procedures should be or where the criteria or cut-off points should be located for deciding what children have special needs. The apparent incidence of learning difficulties is crucially bound up with the assessment procedures, formal and informal, which are applied to children. The relationship between, on the one hand, these procedures and their purposes and, on the other, the consequences for pupils of being assessed as having special needs is a complex one.

Teacher assessments

These difficulties of definition and assessment must affect the way in which classroom teachers come to regard pupils in their class as having special educational needs. The kinds of working definition which teachers will apply will reflect their training, including in-service training, and their classroom experience. Their working definitions are also likely to reflect the personal and institutional situation in which they are working. It has been argued that most assessments of pupils as having special needs inevitably involve some element of comparison with other pupils. The comparisons that are made, however, and that may be tacit rather than explicit in the teacher's mind, may vary considerably. A pupil may be compared with other pupils in the same class, with other pupils of whom the teacher has had experience or with national test norms. Consequently, a child considered as having a learning difficulty in a particular class taught by a particular teacher may not be so considered by a different teacher or in a different class taught by the same teacher.

Other factors likely to influence teacher assessments in addition to their own experience and knowledge and the characteristics of the pupils themselves are those associated with the school and local authority. School and LEA policy and procedures with regard to special educational needs and the availability of support and advice may well influence the view teachers take of their pupils.

The phrase 'special educational needs' logically implies that there is something special which is needed, and the relationship between the assessment of pupils as having special needs and the nature of special provisions is clearly a crucial one. The fact that a child has been assessed as having special educational needs is likely to influence the way teachers view him. For example, the authors of a National Children's Bureau study write:

> A lack of diagnostic and treatment facilities has a curtailing effect on the number of referrals. Conversely, it is a well known phenomenon that if a special school or child clinic is opened there is a steep rise in the number of referrals (Pringle *et al.*, 1966, p. 155).

Consequently, provision for special needs is treated in this report both as something made available in response to such needs and also as a factor influencing the definitions and assessments made of them.

Special needs as a social construct

Our emphasis on assessment as a social process and on special educational needs as an agreed category among practitioners in education differs in a number of crucial respects from that of recent sociological accounts of these processes which have stressed the social functions of assessing children for special education or as having special needs and have argued that systems of special education and assessment ought to be looked at from a sociological point of view rather than in a more traditional way which concentrates on personal characteristics of the children being assessed. Authors such as Tomlinson (1981) and Squibb (1981) have claimed that the system of special education should be seen not in terms of meeting the needs of children in the most appropriate way but in wider sociological and structuralist terms as serving to reproduce a particular social order.

They suggest that special schools and other special provisions exist not to serve best the need of pupils but to remove from the ordinary education system pupils whom schools find unacceptable. They contend that special needs are a socially constructed category and that taking children out of ordinary schools may well be in the

18

interests of the school rather than in the interests of the pupil. In a wider context they argue that the system of special education plays a particular role in perpetuating a social order. They suggest that by labelling and stigmatising pupils in special schools the education system creates a kind of sub-strata of people suitable for low-level manual work who can be readily moved in and out of employment as economic conditions change.

This kind of sociological analysis has a different emphasis from our own recognition that special needs are a social category and that assessment in schools must be understood as a social activity in which a variety of characteristics of pupils, teachers and institutions all have a part to play. We recognise that assessment and allocation procedures are social constructions and that in order to explain them it is necessary to take into account factors other than the overt criteria for categorisation. We also recognise that such procedures can serve latent as well as manifest functions, among which may well be the relieving of pressures on ordinary schools and teachers (although this is usually explicit rather than hidden). Where we differ from the other authors is in refusing to take it for granted that the worst possible motives are the only relevant ones. For example, the fact that it is in an ordinary school's interest to remove a disruptive child to a special unit is not incompatible with its being in the best interest of the child as well. (In making statements of this kind we are concerned in a very limited sense with the best interests of the child in the context of current arrangements for education and special education. We cannot construct a notion of the best possible interests of the child in some kind of ideal world.) We also recognise (and this emerges very clearly from our data collection) that many of the factors described by the authors discussed above are not the dark secrets which they like to suggest. Far from having been discovered by these authors, the range of functions performed by allocation and assessment procedures and the variety of criteria which may be employed are fairly generally recognised by head teachers, educational psychologists, doctors and so on.

The second point made by these authors, implying as it does that the system of special education has a key role to play in social reproduction, seems frankly implausible. It implies that the social structure rests in a key way on a sort of lumpen proletariat sub-structure consisting of the 1 or 2 per cent of the population who end up in special schools. This does not seem very likely, nor is it probable that these people have a key role to play in the economy.

Further, and perhaps more importantly, these accounts fail to do justice to the very real difficulties experienced by some children. As was pointed out earlier, the fact that standardised testing procedures inevitably force some children to be bottom does not mean that these children do not have considerable difficulties. Similarly, the fact that categories of special need are socially created and that the application of them to particular children is imperfect does not mean that the difficulties to which they refer are not real.

There are a minority of children who undoubtedly have educational needs of a special kind. Such children are increasingly the concern of ordinary schools, both because of moves to integrate more children from special schools into ordinary schools and because of a greater awareness of and responsibility for the special needs of other pupils following the Warnock Report and the 1981 legislation. The view teachers take of the difficulties of their pupils, the ways in which pupils come to be regarded as having special educational needs and the consequences of such assessments for schools and children are the focus of the succeeding chapters.

3 The teacher's view of special educational needs in the junior classroom

Using the procedures for sampling and interviewing described in the Appendix it is possible to build up a picture of special educational needs as seen by junior-class teachers. All of the 428 teachers in the survey described any pupils in their classes whom they regarded as having special educational needs and gave details of the difficulties these pupils experienced and presented. The number of children nominated in this way by their teachers, expressed as a proportion of the total number of children in these classes, yields the incidence of special educational needs as perceived by the teachers.

An overview of special educational needs

For the purpose of giving an overview of special educational needs, the descriptions teachers gave of their pupils have been placed in three major categories. The nominated pupils are categorised here in terms of whether or not their teachers described them as having *learning difficulties*, as having *behaviour difficulties* and as having *health-related difficulties* (these including physical handicaps and sensory impairments). The descriptions of pupils could arise either in response to an open-ended question about special educational needs or in response to a specific prompt about particular difficulties. For the present purpose this distinction between prompted and unprompted difficulties is ignored: in fact more than nine out of ten of the pupils discussed by their teachers were nominated in response to the open-ended question.

The overall figures in Table 3.1 show that 18.8 per cent of pupils in the junior classrooms sampled were regarded by their teachers as having special educational needs, that is, five or six children in an average class of twenty-nine or thirty. Learning problems of some

Table 3.1 Special needs in the primary classroom: an overview of teacher assessments

	N	% of nominated pupils	% of all pupils (N = 12310)
All pupils nominated as having special educational needs by 428 junior class teachers	2317	100	18.8
Pupils with learning problems	1898	81.9	15.4
Pupils with behaviour problems	953	41.1	7.7
Pupils with health problems, sensory impairments and physical handicaps	540	23.3	4.5

kind formed by far the largest category of special educational needs. Over four-fifths of the pupils whom their teachers discussed with us had learning difficulties. Of the total sample 15.4 per cent had learning difficulties, that is, four or five pupils in an average class. Behaviour problems of various sorts were about half as frequent as learning difficulties: 7.7 per cent of the total sample, about two children in the average class and four in ten of the pupils discussed by their teachers, were described as having behaviour problems. Health problems and sensory and physical impairments make up the smallest of the major categories used in Table 3.1. Less than one child in twenty in the classes sampled or just under a quarter of the nominated pupils were seen by their teachers as having difficulties of this sort.

As is commonly found in studies of the difficulties and disabilities experienced by children, there is considerable overlap between the major categories presented in Table 3.1. Four out of ten of the pupils nominated by their teachers as having special needs presented difficulties from more than one of the major categories. (This under-estimates the actual prevalence of multiple difficulties as it shows overlap only between the three major categories presented here. There is also overlap within these categories, for example, children having both a health problem and a sensory impairment.) In Table 3.2 the extent of overlap is presented: 28.1 per cent of children nominated as having special needs have both learning problems and behaviour problems; 15.3 per cent have learning problems and health problems; and 9.5 per cent have behaviour problems and health problems. Overlapping these three categories are the 6.5 per cent of pupils with special needs, just over one in a hundred of the total sample of pupils who have all three kinds of difficulty.

Table 3.2 Overlap between broad categories of special educational needs

	N	% of nominated pupils	% of all pupils
Pupils with learning problems only	1043	45.0	8.5
Pupils with behavioural problems only	234	10.1	1.9
Pupils with health and related problems only	117	5.0	1.0
Pupils with learning problems and behaviour problems	651	28.1	5.3
Pupils with learning problems and health problems	355	15.3	2.9
Pupils with behaviour problems and health problems	219	9.5	1.8
Pupils with learning, health and behaviour problems (these pupils are also included in the three rows above)	151	6.5	1.2

These results are presented in a slightly different fashion in Figure 3.1. The total shaded area of the figure shows the proportion of pupils in the junior classrooms regarded by their teachers as having special educational needs. The different combinations of shading in the squares represent the prevalence of different kinds of combinations of special needs. Squares 1, 4 and 6 show children who fall into only one of the categories of special need, squares 2, 3 and 5 show the prevalence

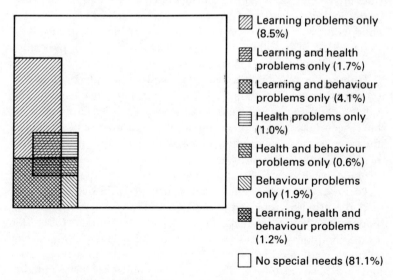

Learning problems only (8.5%)

Learning and health problems only (1.7%)

Learning and behaviour problems only (4.1%)

Health problems only (1.0%)

Health and behaviour problems only (0.6%)

Behaviour problems only (1.9%)

Learning, health and behaviour problems (1.2%)

No special needs (81.1%)

FIGURE 3.1 *Proportions of children with varying combinations of special educational needs*

of overlaps of only two types of special need and square 7 indicates the proportion of pupils who fall into all three categories.

A major point to emerge from these figures is that teacher assessments of pupils with special educational needs result in a pattern of incidence of such needs strikingly similar to the estimate contained in the Warnock Report. The Warnock Committee estimated that about one child in six, that is, between 16 per cent and 17 per cent of pupils, would, at any time, have special needs. The teachers' assessments result in an incidence of 18.8 per cent, between one in six and one in five pupils. The Warnock estimates were based on epidemiological studies of handicap, in particular the major study conducted in the Isle of Wight (Rutter *et al.*, 1970). The overall incidence of special educational needs to emerge from teachers' assessments is close to the overall incidence of 16.6 per cent in the Isle of Wight study. However, the proportion of pupils in particular categories, in particular the proportion of pupils with learning difficulties, is rather higher in the present study than that in the Isle of Wight research. This difference arises because the overlap between types of difficulty is rather greater in the present study, an overlap which suggests that a teacher may be more likely to identify a child as having one kind of difficulty if he has already been identified as having another. For example, it may be that at a particular level of school performance a child who also has behaviour problems is more likely to be identified as having learning difficulties than one who does not. This possibility will be investigated later in the analysis.

It should be noted that comparisons between the categories used in the present research and in the Isle of Wight study are not exact. The categories of 'intellectual retardation' and 'educational backwardness' have been taken as roughly comparable to learning difficulties, and the category 'psychiatric disorder' used in the Isle of Wight study has been taken as equivalent to the general category of 'behaviour problems', which includes discipline problems.

Clearly, any estimates of incidence depend on the definitions used and the criteria employed as well as on the characteristics of the population being studied. Tansley and Pankhurst (1981), for example, quote estimates of the incidence of learning disabilities in various academic and official studies: these estimates range from under 5 per cent to over 20 per cent depending on the population being studied and the way these difficulties are conceptualised. It is striking that the incidence of special needs contained in the Warnock

Report is very similar to the incidence of special needs which emerges when the junior-school teachers in the present study were asked to assess the pupils in their classes. The incidence of special needs relating to learning difficulties as seen by these teachers also parallels the middle range of the estimates discussed by Tansley and Pankhurst. These results give support to the view that there is a consensual notion of what constitutes special needs which could underlie the contribution of ordinary schools and teachers in this area.

However, just as academic estimates depend both on the individuals studied and on the criteria employed, teachers' estimates of the special needs of their pupils will also reflect the way the teacher makes these judgments as well as reflecting the problems experienced by pupils. It is possible that the overall similarity between official estimates of incidence and the estimates which have been presented here disguise considerable variation in the way that individual teachers assess their pupils and apply the notion of learning difficulties and of special educational needs. This will be the focus of later analysis.

Learning difficulties

It has already become apparent that learning difficulties dominate the teachers' view of special educational needs in the junior class-room. Over four-fifths of the pupils described as having special educational needs have learning difficulties of some kind. In Table 3.3 the nature of the learning difficulties described by teachers is presented in more detail. In the pilot study for the present research (Moses, 1982) it was found that the terms 'slow learner' and 'poor reader' were the descriptions most frequently used by teachers to describe children

Table 3.3 *Learning difficulties*

	N	% of learning difficulties	% of all nominations	% of sample
All learning difficulties	1898	100	81.9	15.4
Slow learners	1493	78.7	64.4	12.1
Poor readers	1661	87.5	71.7	13.5
English as a second language	165	8.7	7.1	1.3
Other learning difficulties	146	7.7	6.3	1.2

with learning difficulties, and these were the categories used when the teachers were interviewed in the present study. In addition, a small number of pupils were categorised by the teachers in other ways such as 'under-achieving', 'specific maths problems' or 'handwriting difficulties'. These descriptions were mainly used in addition to the major categories of slow learner and poor reader. There were also a number of children, mainly Asian, whose difficulties are associated with the fact of English not being their first language. These, too, are usually poor readers.

Just as learning difficulties dominated the teacher's view of special educational needs, reading problems were the largest single element of learning difficulties. As Table 3.3 shows, almost nine in ten of the pupils with learning difficulties were described by their teachers as poor readers. These make up 13.5 per cent of the total sample, about four pupils in an average classroom. A lower proportion of the pupils with learning difficulties, though still a substantial majority, were described as slow learners. Nearly four-fifths of those with learning difficulties, 12.1 per cent of the total sample, were described in this way. Other learning difficulties, including ESL problems, listed separately in Table 3.3, account for a relatively small proportion of pupils described as having learning problems.

In Table 3.4 the teachers' perception of reading difficulties as the chief of their pupils' learning problems is again demonstrated. About nine in ten of the pupils described as slow learners or as having ESL difficulties are also described as poor readers. Just over four-fifths of the poor readers and only a half of the ESL problems are also described as slow learners. These results reflect the centrality of reading in the primary classroom both as a tool for achievement in other areas and as a criterion for assessment. As will become apparent later when techniques for formal assessment are described, reading tests are by far the most common form of standardised testing in junior classrooms.

Table 3.4 Overlap between learning difficulties

	Poor readers	Slow learners
% of slow learners who are also:	91.6	100
% of poor readers who are also:	100	82.3
ESL	89.7	50.9
Other	24.0	37.3

Problems associated with behaviour

In considering the overall picture of special educational needs as seen by junior-school teachers, one of the major categories used was that of 'behaviour problems'. Over four in ten of the pupils described by their teachers as having special educational needs, that is, 7.7 per cent of all the pupils in the study, were described by their teachers as having special needs associated with behavioural difficulties. Very often these pupils also had other difficulties. Over two-thirds of them were also described by their teachers as having learning difficulties and nearly a quarter had physical or sensory disabilities or health problems. Only a quarter of the children with behaviour problems were seen by their teachers as having this as their only special educational need.

It was found in the pilot study (Moses, 1982) that most teachers made a distinction between behaviour which created difficulties for the child and behaviour which created difficulties for the teacher in terms of classroom control. This distinction was made in obtaining teacher descriptions of special educational needs associated with behaviour, and teachers again distinguished between pupils with behavioural or emotional difficulties and pupils who presented discipline problems in the classroom, although, of course, in practice these types of behaviour overlap considerably. As Table 3.5 shows, the great majority of children who were described by their teachers as having special needs associated with behaviour were seen as being

Table 3.5 Behavioural/emotional and discipline problems

	N	% of nominated pupils	% of all pupils
All nominated behavioural/emotional and discipline problems	953	41.1	7.7
Behavioural/emotional problems	872	37.6	7.1
Discipline problems	500	21.6	4.1
Behavioural/emotional and discipline problems	419	18.1	3.4

N.B. Of the 872 pupils with behavioural/emotional problems, 419 or 48.1 per cent are also discipline problems.

Of the 500 pupils described as discipline problems, 419 or 83.8 per cent are also described as behavioural/emotional problems.

Of the total of 953 pupils with behavioural/emotional or discipline problems, 651 or 68.3 per cent also have learning difficulties.

behaviourally or emotionally disturbed. Just under half of these pupils were also described by their teachers as presenting a discipline problem. It is clear that, contrary to what has been sometimes suggested (e.g. Herbert, 1975), teachers do not identify difficulties of a behavioural and emotional kind only when such difficulties present an overt problem of classroom control. Over half of the children described by their teachers as having behavioural difficulties were not seen as posing a problem of discipline.

There are, however, a number of pupils who do pose problems of classroom discipline. Five hundred pupils, 4.1 per cent of all the children in the study and just over a fifth of all pupils described as having special educational needs, were described by their teachers as discipline problems. The great majority of these children, 83.8 per cent, were seen by their teachers as also being behaviourally or emotionally disturbed. A small proportion of the children with discipline problems were described by their teachers as posing problems in the classroom because of their 'naughtiness' but were not regarded as exhibiting behavioural or emotional disturbance.

Behavioural and emotional difficulties and the problems of class-room control which are sometimes associated with such difficulties form a substantial group among the special educational needs described by junior-school teachers. Difficulties of this kind are attributed, on average, to over two children per class. Most of these children are seen by their teachers as presenting behavioural and emotional disturbances and about a half of them pose discipline problems for the teacher. Behavioural disturbances and discipline problems are strongly related, but just over half the pupils described as behaviourally and emotionally disturbed do not pose problems of discipline, and there are a few pupils who do pose discipline problems but are not regarded by their teachers as exhibiting behavioural or emotional disturbances.

Physical handicaps, sensory impairments and health problems

Just under a quarter of the pupils described by their teachers as having special educational needs had health-related problems of some sort, including physical handicaps and sensory impairments. This amounts to just under one in twenty of the pupils in the classes in the survey. Two-thirds of these children were also described as having learning difficulties, and two-fifths were described as having problems associated with behaviour. Only 21.6 per cent of the children with health-related difficulties did not have learning or behavioural problems.

The problem of identifying health-related difficulties and in relating them to other difficulties experienced by a child was one of which teachers were very conscious and where they often felt unsure of themselves. In contrast to other difficulties, in particular learning problems and discipline problems, which arise very directly from the teachers' professional responsibilities and experience of a child in the classroom, health-related problems lie outside the normal professional skills of the teachers. Moreover, not only does the extent to which health problems are educationally relevant vary, but so too does the teacher's awareness of health-related difficulties that may be affecting a child's response to schooling. A number of teachers reported instances where parents or the school medical services had failed to tell them about medical difficulties experienced by a child, and teachers were sometimes unsure whether such difficulties were associated with the learning and behaviour problems children displayed.

Table 3.6 Physical handicaps, sensory impairments and health problems

	N	% of nominated pupils	% of all pupils
Children with physical handicaps	101	4.4	0.8
Children with hearing impairments	133	5.7	1.1
Children with sight impairments	89	3.8	0.7
Children with speech impairments	71	3.1	0.6
Children with other health difficulties	228	9.8	1.9
All children with physical, sensory or health problems	540	23.3	4.4

In view of this, the detailed list of teachers' descriptions of health-related difficulties presented in Table 3.6 must be treated more cautiously as estimates of incidence than the descriptions of learning and behavioural problems presented earlier. Teachers identified 0.8 per cent of pupils in their classes as having a physical handicap of some sort, 1.1 per cent as having hearing difficulties, 0.7 per cent as having sight difficulties and 0.6 per cent as having a speech impairment. A further 1.9 per cent of pupils had other health problems; these included asthma, eczema and suspected undernourishment as well as more short-term illnesses. Of the 4.4 per cent of the total sample (or 23.3. per cent of the nominated pupils) having such problems, the great majority, nearly four in five, also had problems connected with learning, behaviour or both.

Variations in special educational needs by sex and age level of pupils

The results presented so far have dealt with special educational needs in terms of the average level of such needs across all teachers and pupils. As will be shown later in this chapter, the number of pupils identified as having such needs varied from teacher to teacher and school to school. Further variation was found, however, in the perceived incidence of special educational needs among children of different sub-groups in the total sample of children. In the present section variations will be considered according to sex and age level of pupils. Each child identified by a teacher as having a special educational need was also classified along these two dimensions. From each school the total number was obtained of boy and girl

Table 3.7 *Special educational needs and sex of pupils*

	Boys %	Girls %
All special educational needs	24.4	13.2
Learning difficulties	19.5	11.1
Behaviour problems	10.9	4.5
Health problems	5.8	2.9
Slow learners	15.5	8.8
Poor readers	17.5	9.5
ESL	1.4	1.2
Behavioural/emotional problems	10.1	4.1
Discipline problems	6.4	1.7
N =	6275	6035

pupils and of pupils in each year group. Using these data it is possible to consider the incidence of special educational needs separately for the various groups.

In Table 3.7 teacher nominations of boys and girls are compared both with respect to the three major categories of special needs and also for some more detailed categories of particular interest. The ratio of boys to girls among the nominated pupils is almost two to one, a result similar to the findings of epidemiological studies of such difficulties (Rutter, Tizard and Whitmore, 1970, Pringle *et al.*, 1966). Learning difficulties are attributed to 19.5 per cent of boys and 11.1 per cent of girls, behavioural difficulties to 10.9 per cent of boys and 4.5 per cent of girls and health and related problems to 5.8 per cent of boys and 2.9 per cent of girls. The most dramatic difference is in the category of discipline problems, where boys outnumber girls by almost four to one. Overall, 24.4 per cent of boys are described as having special educational needs compared with 13.2 per cent of girls.

Table 3.8 shows the incidence of special educational needs in four different age groups from first-year juniors to fourth-year juniors. It

Table 3.8 Special educational needs and ages of pupils

	1st yrs %	2nd yrs %	3rd yrs %	4th yrs %
All special educational needs	21.1	19.5	18.3	16.4
Learning difficulties	17.8	16.1	14.7	13.2
Behaviour problems	8.2	7.6	7.9	7.2
Health problems	5.5	4.6	3.7	3.9
Slow learners	14.1	12.4	12.1	9.9
Poor readers	16.1	14.9	12.4	10.7
ESL	1.6	1.4	1.1	1.3
Behavioural/emotional problems	7.6	6.9	7.3	6.6
Discipline problems	3.7	3.9	4.3	4.3
N =	2832	3001	3234	3243

will be seen that, as the age of the children increases, the proportion of them identified as having special educational needs steadily declines: 21.2 per cent of the youngest age group are identified as having special educational needs compared with 16.4 per cent of the oldest age group. For the most part these differences are due to a decrease in the proportion of pupils having learning difficulties. The incidence of learning difficulties declines from 17.8 per cent to 13.2 per cent across the four years, while the incidence of behavioural problems declines from 8.2 per cent to 7.2 per cent and the incidence of health-related problems from 5.5 per cent to 3.9 per cent. The decline in health-related difficulties is partly due to a dramatic decrease among the older children in the proportion of pupils with speech impairments.

The decrease in the proportion of pupils identified by the teachers as having learning difficulties may be associated with the timing of transferrals from ordinary school to special schools, especially to ESN(M) schools, which typically occurs during the junior school years. Some of the pupils identified as having learning difficulties in the first and second year of junior schooling will be transferred into special schools as they become older and would therefore not be in ordinary classes to be identified in the later years of the junior school. However, part of the explanation may also be that teachers apply different criteria for learning difficulties to children of different ages. It may be, for example, that in the early stages children are regarded as poor readers when their difficulties, relative to other children, are less severe than children's difficulties so regarded at a later stage in their school life. Children of seven who are well behind their chronological age are virtual non-readers, while children of eleven may be substantially behind but nevertheless have basic reading skills, an acquisition which may have considerable implications for the way in which the child can cope with a variety of classroom activities. It is probable that a non-reading first-year junior will appear much more 'lost' in the classroom than a fourth-year pupil of poor reading ability even when their achievements relative to their respective ages are similar. The point is made speculatively here but will be taken up again in the analysis of the relationship of test results to teacher nominations in Chapter 6.

Ethnic minority pupils and teacher assessments of special educational needs

The question of the assessment of the special educational needs of pupils from ethnic minority backgrounds and the proportion of such children regarded as having special educational needs as a result of these assessments is particularly difficult and sometimes controversial.

This is especially so in the case of children from West Indian backgrounds.* There is evidence that children of West Indian origin perform less well on standardised tests of achievement and ability than do other pupils, and some reason to believe that they are over-represented among children in ESN(M) special schools (Taylor, 1982, Coard, 1971, Tomlinson, 1981). Although children from Asian backgrounds also have special needs those needs are frequently connected with the problem of English not being a first language. The difficulties which West Indian pupils experience in the British school system do not have such an obvious explanation as the language difficulties of Asian pupils and have become a politically sensitive and controversial issue in education.

A recent review of research conducted by the NFER has looked at a large number of studies in this area (Taylor, 1982). These studies, for the most part, document the poorer average performance of children of West Indian origin although one recent study has found a higher level of examination passes among such children, especially girls (Driver, 1980). A variety of explanations have been offered for this general lower average level of performance. These have included the effects of social deprivation and other aspects of family circumstances and also the often unacknowledged linguistic differences between West Indian speech forms and standard English. Other authors have rejected what they see as an attempt to blame the West Indian child and his family for the inadequacies of schools and have looked instead for explanatory factors in terms of the operation of the educational system and the wider society. These explanations see racism as a crucial factor and suggest that racially biased assessment procedures and racially discriminatory stereotypes on the part of teachers and others are responsible for the difficulties children of West Indian origin experience (e.g. Tomlinson, 1981, Coard, 1971). Attempts to carry out research on these issues have run into difficulties both

---

* The description of differences between ethnic groups poses problems of terminology. Many (probably most) of the children from ethnic minorities in the sample were born in Britain and are as 'indigenous' as the rest of the sample. In this discussion children from families of Caribbean origin will be referred to as West Indian or of West Indian origin. Children from families who have come from the Indian sub-continent (including those who have come via East Africa) will be referred to as Asian or of Asian origin. Other children (with the exception of a few children from Chinese, Arabic or African backgrounds who have not been included in the analysis of ethnic minority groups) will be referred to as white.

because of the considerable methodological problems and because of political sensitivity.

These issues are obviously important in considering the special educational needs of ethnic minority children, especially those of West Indian origin. The Warnock Report does not really confront this problem beyond noting with concern that West Indian children may make up a disproportionate number of children in special schools, although the Report does emphasise that assessments of children's special educational needs should be sensitive to cultural differences (DES, 1978, p. 64).

The present research was not designed to look specifically at the special educational needs of pupils from ethnic minority backgrounds nor to examine factors which might explain any over-representation of particular ethnic groups among children with special educational needs. Thus, children from Asian and West Indian homes (and a few children from other ethnic minority backgrounds) appear in the data as a reflection of their distribution in schools and not as a reflection of a specific sampling strategy. No special information was collected about them and the teachers were not asked about any special difficulties which arose from teaching in multi-cultural classrooms. Nevertheless, it is possible to calculate the proportions of children from different ethnic backgrounds described as having different sorts of special needs. (It is also possible to look at differences in the teachers' descriptions of the causes of these difficulties for children from different ethnic groups, and these results are presented in Chapter 4. The test data do not differentiate children by ethnic group and so no comparison of test performances is possible. Because the numbers of children from ethnic minorities in the observational study are very small, no conclusions can be drawn from these results.) Consequently, the results which are presented here simply deal with the differences in proportions of children from different ethnic backgrounds regarded by their teachers as having special educational needs. These results should be treated very cautiously. They may reflect differences in characteristics of the children, from whatever cause, or they may reflect differences in teacher perceptions and expectations. In view of the problem discussed above and the claims made about the way in which West Indian children are treated in the English educational system it is important to be clear that the present study was not designed to address these issues.

As can be seen in the first part of Table 3.9, children from ethnic

Table 3.9 Special educational needs by sex and ethnic group

	All pupils			Boys			Girls		
	White	Asian	West Indian	White	Asian	West Indian	White	Asian	West Indian
	%	%	%	%	%	%	%	%	%
All special educational needs	18.0	24.1	24.2	23.4	24.4	35.0	12.4	23.7	13.1
Learning difficulties	14.6	22.0	18.4	18.9	22.2	25.0	10.0	21.7	11.7
Behaviour problems	7.8	4.7	16.6	10.8	6.3	25.0	4.5	2.8	8.0
Health problems	4.5	3.1	5.1	5.8	3.9	9.3	3.1	2.2	0.7
Slow learners	11.9	13.4	16.6	15.1	13.1	22.1	8.5	13.8	10.9
Poor readers	12.9	17.8	14.8	16.8	18.5	20.7	8.9	17.0	8.9
ESL	0.1	13.4	0	0.1	13.1	0	0.1	13.8	0
Behavioural/ emotional problems	7.2	4.1	13.7	9.9	5.4	21.4	4.2	2.6	5.8
Discipline problems	4.0	1.9	14.1	6.2	3.0	21.4	1.7	0.6	6.6
N =	11004	1005	277	5595	540	140	5409	465	137

minority backgrounds are more likely than the rest of the sample to be described as having special educational needs. Just over 24 per cent of both Asian and West Indian pupils were described as having special needs compared with 18 per cent of the white pupils. Asian pupils are especially likely to have learning problems while West Indian pupils are seen as having greater learning problems than the white children but fewer than the Asians. Asian pupils on the other hand, when compared with the other two groups, are under-represented among children with behaviour problems while West Indian children are over-represented. More detail of these results is given in the bottom half of the first part of Table 3.9. The special nature of the learning difficulties of Asian pupils is apparent here. Asian children are particularly likely to have reading problems, mainly associated with the fact that English is not their first language. Despite these difficulties they are only slightly more likely than white pupils to be described as slow learners. In contrast, the West Indian pupils are particularly likely to be described as slow learners but produce a similar proportion of poor readers to the white children. Children of West Indian origin are the only group among whom the proportion described as slow learners is higher than that described as poor readers. These children are also very much more likely than the other groups to be described as discipline problems.

Also presented in Table 3.9 are the differences between boys and girls within the different ethnic groups. This analysis shows the special nature of the difficulties of the Asian children. In the sample as a whole, boys outnumber girls among the children described as having special needs in a ratio of about two to one. For the Asian pupils, however, the proportion of boys having any sort of special needs and having learning difficulties is very little higher than the proportion of girls. This suggests that their difficulties have, in part, a different source. In the other groups, being a boy is associated with a much stronger likelihood of having special educational needs. Among children of Asian origin this is not so, and the suggestion is that the language problems which boys and girls have in common are a major factor in their special needs.

Among the West Indian children the boys outnumber the girls just as they do for white children. However, in the case of the West Indians the difference between boys and girls is even greater so that the over-representation of West Indian children is principally an over-representation of West Indian boys. West Indian girls are very similar to white girls in the overall proportion described as having special needs and as having learning problems. They are, however, somewhat higher in the proportion described as having behaviour problems and considerably higher on the count of discipline problems.

Table 3.9 shows that, at the level of teacher perception, West Indian boys are more likely to be seen as slow learners and West Indian boys and girls are more likely to be seen as behaviour problems and, particularly, as discipline problems. Among Asian children, in contrast to the other two groups, boys and girls are seen as having similar levels of learning difficulty. They differ with regard to behaviour problems, with the boys seen as outnumbering the girls in a similar fashion to the other groups. Both boys and girls, however, have lower levels of behaviour and discipline problems than the pupils from other ethnic groups.

These results have been presented in terms of the differences between the different ethnic groups but attention should also be drawn to the overall similarity between the groups of children in their special educational needs. The differences are very much smaller than, for example, the differences between boys and girls. The results show, in common with other studies, the difficulties that some children from West Indian backgrounds have in the English educational system, but they also indicate that these difficulties are basically similar to those of other pupils. They also show that the great majority of pupils in all the ethnic groups are not seen by their teachers as having special difficulties and that special needs are experienced by a minority of children from all the groups.

Variation in special needs across schools and classes

The pattern of variation in the incidence of special educational needs from class to class and from school to school raises a number of interesting questions. First, there is the question of whether special needs should be regarded as a problem for schools generally. It is well established that children from disadvantaged social backgrounds are particularly at risk with regard to educational failure, behavioural disturbance and health difficulties, and that, more generally, the incidence of such difficulties is correlated with the child's socio-economic background. (See for example Pringle *et al.*, 1966, pp. 114–47, and Townsend and Davidson, 1982.) If schools tend to draw on relatively homogeneous catchment areas it may be that special educational needs will be heavily concentrated in certain schools and virtually non-existent in others. This would have considerable implications for any policy towards special needs, for it would mean that the Warnock Report's suggestion that 'a teacher of a mixed-ability class . . . should be aware that . . . about four or five of them may require special educational provision at any given time' is misleading as a general suggestion to teachers.

In Tables 3.10 and 3.11 schools and then teachers are classified according to the proportions of their pupils who are nominated as having special educational needs. Table 3.10 gives an overall view of these proportions, while Table 3.11 looks in detail at the lower end of the distribution. The pattern to emerge is one of variation between schools in the numbers of pupils seen by their teachers as having special needs, with, however, no tendency for schools to divide into those that have and those that lack pupils with problems. More than seven in ten of the schools in the study regarded between 10 per cent and 30 per cent of their pupils as having special needs. Four of the sixty-one schools in the study had more than 30 per cent of pupils with special needs but no school had as many as half of their pupils falling

Table 3.10 *Variation in the proportion of pupils having special needs across schools and teachers*

Proportions of pupils nominated as having special needs	Schools		Teachers	
	N	%	N	%
10% and below	13	21.3	92	21.5
10%–20%	26	42.6	138	32.2
20%–30%	18	29.5	115	26.8
30%–40%	2	3.3	52	12.1
40%–50%	2	3.3	25	5.8
50% +	0	—	6	1.4
	61	100.0	428	100.0

Table 3.11 *Distribution of very low proportions of special needs by schools and teachers*

	Schools		Teachers	
	N	%	N	%
No special needs	0	—	15	3.5
5% or fewer special needs but greater than zero	1	1.6	31	7.2
	1	1.6	46	10.7

into this category. At the other end of the distribution just over one in five of the schools had 10 per cent or fewer pupils with special educational needs, but in only one school did this fall to 5 per cent or below, and no school was without pupils with special needs. These figures indicate that schools vary considerably in the extent of difficulties their pupils experience but also that special educational needs are a general problem for the school system and are not concentrated in a few problem schools.

Related to this question of the distribution across schools of children with special needs is the question of the variation in the proportions of their classes that teachers nominate as having special educational needs. Clearly the distribution of children with difficulties of various sorts is not likely to be even between classes, both because of differences in the characteristics of the schools and their catchment areas and because of the random variation which is bound to occur in the composition of relatively small groups such as a school class. Nevertheless, it is possible that teachers will perceive special educational needs in a relatively uniform way, that is, they may regard a fairly constant proportion of their class as having special needs (judged relative to the rest of the class) whatever the actual level of difficulties experienced by pupils. If this is indeed the case we would expect to find that all teachers nominate about one in six of their class as having special educational needs but that the actual nature of these children's difficulties will vary dramatically from class to class. As Tables 3.10 and 3.11 show, however, this does not in fact seem to be the case. The range of proportions of pupils with special needs across classes is very much greater than the range across schools. Six in ten of the teachers interviewed regarded between 10 per cent and 30 per cent of their classes as having special needs, but fifteen teachers (3.5 per cent) had no children in their classes whom they regarded as having special needs, and six teachers (1.4 per cent) regarded over half of their class as having special needs. More than one teacher in ten nominated 5 per cent or fewer of their class (never more than one child) as having special needs, while only one school out of the sixty-one had 5 per cent or fewer pupils with special needs. At the other end of the scale 7.2 per cent of the teachers nominated more than 40 per cent of their class, while only 3.3 per cent of schools had this sort of proportion. The question of the relationship between the overall characteristics of the class and teachers' perceptions of special educational needs will be dealt with in detail later in the analysis, but these results, although they show there is a clustering of teachers in the middle range of nominations, provide no evidence that teachers see a fixed proportion of their class as having special needs.

Provision

When teachers were describing the pupils they had nominated as having special educational needs, they were asked about any extra help the child was receiving and about any further help which they would like the child to receive. These results will be presented in detail in Chapter 8, but there is one aspect of the answers to these questions which is relevant to the question under present consideration, of the incidence of special educational needs. In the case of just over one in five of the pupils described as having special educational needs the child was not receiving any extra help, nor did the teacher want such help for the child. A higher proportion of pupils with behavioural and health problems fell into this category than did pupils with learning difficulties, but all kinds of pupils were included.

This partial mismatch between identified needs and the requirement for provision raises the question of what is understood by special educational needs. In the sense the Warnock Report gives the phrase, a sense adopted in the 1981 Education Act, a special educational need is a need for some sort of provision. In the case of the majority of children this usage was implicitly adopted by teachers, in that need was seen as the need for provision. For a minority of children, however, it seems that teachers are applying current terminology but thinking of children in a more traditional fashion in terms of their deficiencies and disabilities rather than in terms of their needing some sort of special provision.

Summary: the incidence of special educational needs

When teachers of junior classes are asked to describe pupils in their class with special educational needs, 18.8 per cent, between five and six children in an average class, are nominated. Four-fifths of these children have learning difficulties of some kind, two-fifths have behavioural difficulties and just under a quarter have health problems, including physical handicaps and sensory impairments. These figures make it clear that many children must have multiple difficulties. In fact, four out of ten of the children discussed by their teachers had problems that fall into more than one of the major categories of learning, behaviour and health. In particular, two-thirds of the children described as having behavioural and/or health-related difficulties also had learning problems.

The overall incidence of special educational needs that emerges from these figures and the predominance of learning problems within them provide a very similar picture to the estimates included in the Warnock Report, estimates on which the broad concept of special educational needs introduced in the Report was based. This similarity suggests that, despite the difficulties of definition implicit in the concept of special educational needs, there is at least the basis for a consensual agreement between professionals involved in education with regard to the application of the 'broad concept'. It is also clear that special educational needs are seen by teachers as being relatively widely spread throughout the educational system and are not restricted to a few 'problem' schools, a finding which again confirms the Warnock view that these difficulties are of concern to all school teachers.

Within this overall pattern of similarity between teachers' views of special educational needs and the estimates contained in the Warnock Report there is, nevertheless, considerable variation between individual teachers in the proportions of their classes described as having such needs. This variation will, at least in part, reflect variations in the actual characteristics of pupils in these classes, and in subsequent analysis the relationship between characteristics of pupils as described by tests of achievement and classroom observation will be related to teacher assessments. In later chapters we shall be concerned both with characteristics which are directly relevant to the assessments being made and also with characteristics which may mislead teachers in their assessments. Variation between teachers may reflect not only differences between the pupils being assessed, but also differences in the way that different teachers regard special educational needs. Assessments will therefore be related not only to characteristics of pupils, but also to characteristics of teachers which may be relevant to variations in assessment.

4 Teachers' views on the aetiology of special educational needs

Teachers' ideas about the causes of special needs, particularly learning difficulties and behaviour problems, are likely to affect the attitudes they take towards children with special needs and so to influence the ways in which they react towards them in the classroom. When considering teachers' explanations of the special needs of their pupils it is of interest to set them in the context of the different, and at times competing, explanations available for children's academic failures and behavioural difficulties. A major theme of social scientific discussions of the causes underlying the academic success and failure of pupils has been the question of the relative importance of the child's innate qualities, particularly those associated with intelligence, and the environment in which a child finds himself, particularly those aspects of the environment associated with the social and economic circumstances of his family. A more recent theme of educational research has been the degree and type of impact of the school and the teacher on children's achievement and behaviour. Also related to explanations which emphasise the role of the school and teacher is the growing popularity of behaviourally-based techniques for influencing children's learning and behaviour.

Environment and innate qualities

The sorts of explanation for children's achievements and behaviour with which teachers are most likely to be familiar derive from the tradition of concern over the relative influence of the home environment and of children's innate qualities. This issue was considered, for example, by Sir Cyril Burt in 'The Causes and Treatment of Backwardness' and 'The Young Delinquent', which regarded both innate potential and home circumstances as causal factors in educational backwardness and behaviour problems. Researchers concerned with the criteria for and effects of selection at 11+ for different types of secondary education were concerned to show that not only measured IQ but also a child's socio-economic background influenced his success in the selection process (e.g. Floud and Halsey, 1957, and Halsey and Gardiner, 1953). Studies such as those of the National Children's Bureau (Pringle *et al.*, 1966) describe the relationship of a complex structure of medical and intellectual factors to children's achievements as well as relating these factors to children's home conditions.

These approaches also dominate the influential report of the Plowden Committee, 'Children and their Primary Schools' (DES, 1967). The first substantive chapter of this report is entitled 'The Children, their Growth and Development' and is concerned with developmental differences among children, factors affecting physical and emotional development and the measurement of intelligence. Following this is a section headed 'The Home, School and Neighbourhood', which is concerned with the effect of children's environment on the school. In considering the impact of environment the Plowden Report differs from some of the earlier studies in putting particular emphasis on the effect of parental attitudes towards education as opposed to the effects of the physical or material circumstances of the home on children.

The school

Causal influences on pupils' school performance deriving from their innate characteristics or from their home circumstances or from interactions between these are, of course, outside the control of the teacher. It is undoubtedly helpful for the teacher to know of the influence of such factors but such recognition will not necessarily produce changes in teaching methods. More recently, research has tended to concentrate on factors of possible causal relevance to pupils' academic performances which are within the control or influence of the school or of the teacher. This approach to research is concerned with more directly educational influences rather than social and psychological influences in the broader sense. For example, research in England such as the Lancaster Study (Bennett, 1976) and the ORACLE research conducted at the University of Leicester (Galton and Croll, 1980) have both concluded that the teaching methods used by primary school teachers have a systematic influence on classes of pupils, so that classes taught in some ways progress at a faster rate than classes taught in others. The research of Professor Rutter and his colleagues (Rutter *et al.*, 1979) has suggested that the influence exerted by the ethos of a school on its pupils can affect their academic progress, their behaviour and their school attendance. Similar research in the United States has concluded that some teachers do elicit better academic performance than others and that this is systematically related to the teaching methods they adopt (Brophy, 1979).

Other developments have concentrated on the way that teachers can ameliorate the behavioural and academic difficulties of pupils with special educational needs. For example, use of techniques based on behaviour modification enables teachers to make careful and precise descriptions of the behavioural changes they want to effect in children and to structure a system of rewards in order to do so (Merrett and Wheldall, 1978, Presland, 1976). Parallel approaches to helping children with academic difficulties sometimes called 'precision teaching' involve breaking down academic tasks into small steps and setting very explicit criteria for children's achievements. By means of measuring children's progress on carefully specified tasks on a day-to-day basis it is possible to get immediate feedback on the effectiveness of teaching approaches and to modify them as appropriate (Ainscoe and Tweddle, 1979, Williams, Muncey and Winteringham, 1980).

Developments of this sort, in common with the research on teaching methods described earlier, do not deny the importance of background factors of various kinds in explaining children's difficulties and achievements. But, having accepted the importance of such factors, they go on to look at further influences on pupils' performance and behaviour, particularly influences which are under the control of the school and the teacher. From the descriptions of pupils given by their teachers in response to questions about causal factors in special educational needs it is possible to construct the various causal explanations for different types of special educational needs which most readily occur to teachers.

Teachers' views

It is of particular interest to contrast three different broad categories of explanation: explanations which refer to factors 'within' a child, explanations referring to characteristics of the child's home background or parents and explanations which refer to characteristics of the school, the teacher or the teaching methods. In Table 4.1a the teachers' explanations of their pupils' special educational needs are coded according to more detailed categories which can then be collapsed into these broad categories. Separate explanations were elicited of all difficulties to do with learning and behaviour mentioned by the teachers. In Table 4.1b these results are summarised according to the three broad categories. All explanations offered by the teachers were coded, and quite often more than one explanation was available for a particular type of difficulty.

Under the general heading of 'within-child' factors are included 'IQ or ability', 'attitude' and 'concentration', as well as interactions of within-child factors or a generalised indication that the difficulties were innate. Health difficulties and physical and sensory defects were not included as within-child factors but were coded separately, as was absence from school, which sometimes accompanied health difficulties. Causal factors connected with the home or the child's parents were coded together whether these were to do with material circumstances, parental attitudes or pathological social or emotional conditions. Causal factors connected with the school or the teacher were coded separately in terms of whether they were ascribed to the present school and the present teacher or to a previous school or a previous teacher. Two other causal factors were found, which, like health and absence, did not fit into the three broad categories: these were behavioural problems to which learning and reading difficulties were sometimes ascribed and, conversely, learning and reading difficulties which were said to cause behaviour problems. The fact that English was not the home language was sometimes given as a causal factor, particularly for learning problems.

The first point to emerge from Table 4.1 is that, in general, teachers do have available to them explanations of a causal kind to account for the difficulties of children in their class: for almost nine out of ten of the difficulties described the teachers were prepared to offer a causal explanation. The second major point is that teachers' explanations are dominated by factors related to children's innate qualities and the

45

Table 4.1 Teachers' explanations of their pupils' special educational needs

Table 4.1a Causal factors

	Slow learner %	Poor reader %	Behaviour/ emotional problem %	Discipline problem %
		Type of difficulty		
IQ/ability	43.8[1]	35.4	1.6	1.2
Attitude	8.5	8.6	6.7	11.0
Lack of concentration	5.1	5.1	5.6	9.6
Generalised 'within-child'[2]	19.0	19.5	17.6	21.0
Other 'within-child'	2.4	2.7	2.3	0.6
Health and physical handicaps	2.6	2.1	1.9	1.4
Absence	3.8	4.5	0.7	0.2
Home/parents	29.8	30.4	65.8	65.6
School/teacher	1.8	2.1	2.1	3.4
Other school/other teacher	1.3	1.3	0.5	0.4
Behaviour	3.8	4.0	—	—
Reading problems	1.9	0.3[3]	1.1	1.2
Learning problems	—	1.1	1.8	1.2
ESL	3.8	5.8	0.3	0.8
Other	1.0	2.0	0.1	0.2
Don't know	9.0	10.6	16.3	13.6

1 All figures are percentages of the total pupils having a particular kind of difficulty for whom their teachers offered a particular explanation. For example, in the case of 43.8 per cent of the pupils described as slow learners their teachers attributed this at least in part to IQ/ability.

2 This category was used when a teacher described difficulties as being due either to ability or attitude or to a possible combination of these.

3 These children are those whose reading problems were explicitly described by their teachers as resulting from dyslexia.

Table 4.1b Summary of causal factors

Any 'within-child' (not including health)	70.5	64.8	30.8	38.8
Home	29.8	30.4	65.8	65.6
Any school/teacher	3.2	3.4	2.5	3.8
Any health/absence	6.2	6.4	2.6	1.6
Any 'within-child' or home factors	82.6	78.4	80.3	82.4
N =	1492	1660	872	500

characteristics of their home and parents rather than to characteristics of their schools and teachers and the teaching methods that are used.

Factors innate to the child (not including health difficulties and sensory and physical defects) are said to be causally relevant to the difficulties of 70.5 per cent of the pupils described as slow learners, to 64.8 per cent of pupils described as poor readers, to 30.8 per cent of pupils with behavioural and emotional difficulties and to 38.8 per cent of children described as discipline problems. In the case of children with learning and reading difficulties the largest component of these innate factors is said to be the child's IQ or ability, followed by more generalised innate factors and factors to do with attitude and concentration. In the case of children with behavioural or discipline problems it is the generalised innate within-child factors which are seen as most important, followed by attitudinal factors and lack of concentration. The child's home circumstances or characteristics of his parents are said to be causally relevant to the difficulties of 29.8 per cent of children described as slow learners, 30.4 per cent of poor readers, 65.8 per cent of behaviour or emotional problems and 65.6 per cent of discipline problems.

In contrast to these two very substantial categories, characteristics of the school and the teacher are seen as being causally relevant to difficulties in only a small minority of cases. In the case of only 3.2 per cent of the slow learners, 3.4 per cent of the poor readers, 2.5 per cent of behaviour and emotional problems and 3.8 per cent of discipline problems did the teacher say that he or she thought that the child's difficulties were caused either by his present school or teachers or by previous schools or teachers.

The picture presented by the teachers is that learning problems generally are seen as very likely to be caused by innate characteristics of the child, with a substantial minority of cases having causal factors related to the home and the parents. In contrast, behavioural and discipline problems are seen as in the main deriving from the home and parental circumstances of the child. With both kinds of difficulty there is, of course, a good deal of overlap between these causal factors. The teachers attributed about four in five of the difficulties they discussed, and about nine in ten of the difficulties for which they are prepared to offer explanations, to either a child's innate characteristics or his home and parents, sometimes to both factors. By contrast, only about three in a hundred of the difficulties discussed are seen as deriving from the school or the teacher.

A similar tendency to attribute difficulties to factors other than the teachers and the school emerged when heads were asked about the situation with regard to special educational needs in their schools. Of the fifty-eight heads interviewed twenty-five said that their school had an above-average proportion of pupils with difficulties of various kinds. When they were asked about the reasons for this only one head said that it was connected with the school, while twenty-four mentioned characteristics of the catchment area or characteristics of parents. Not surprisingly, heads were more inclined to attribute a below-average proportion of pupils with special needs to school factors, although this still accounted for less than a third of such heads. Of the twenty-two heads who said that their schools had a below-average proportion of children with difficulties, seven mentioned characteristics of the school as causal factors and sixteen mentioned characteristics of the catchment area and the pupils' homes.

These results are not surprising given the heavy concentration both on factors innate to the child and on the effects of the home environment in academic research on children's performance and difficulties and in official reports such as those of the Plowden Committee. The results show that teachers are very familiar with explanations of this sort and apply them readily to children in their classes. Other explanations, which emphasise school and classroom as powerful influences on children's behaviour, are much less familiar to teachers and thus very much less likely to be invoked when individual children are discussed. Explanations of this latter sort are not more true or more valid than explanations in terms of individual or social pathology and certainly do not contradict them. They do, however, offer an additional insight into the reasons for the difficulties children experience and suggest causal factors which may be more amenable to influence on the part of schools and teachers and which are, therefore, in some ways more relevant educationally.

Teachers' explanations for special educational needs among different ethnic groups

In Table 4.2 the teachers' views on the causes of pupils' special educational needs are shown separately for the different ethnic groups. The main point to emerge from these results is that Asian children's

Table 4.2 Teachers' explanations of their pupils' special educational needs by ethnic groups

	'White' pupils %	Pupils of Asian origin %	Pupils of West Indian origin %
Slow learner			
'Within-child'	73.3	50.4	80.4
Home/parent	29.9	31.1	50.0
School/teacher	3.3	2.2	4.3
N =	1307	135	46
Poor reader			
'Within-child'	69.0	36.9	75.6
Home/parent	30.3	30.7	46.3
School/teacher	3.7	2.2	4.9
N =	1419	179	41
Behaviour			
'Within-child'	32.1	7.3	36.8
Home/parent	67.0	56.1	73.7
School/teacher	2.4	2.4	5.3
N =	787	41	38
Discipline			
'Within-child'	39.4	15.8	46.2
Home/parent	66.7	63.2	69.2
School/teacher	3.9	—	5.1
N =	439	19	39

difficulties are 'under-explained' in terms of the categories of 'within-child' and home/parent factors and that West Indian children's difficulties are 'over-explained'. Asian pupils are recognised by teachers to have specific difficulties arising from relative unfamiliarity with English and are less likely than the white pupils to have their difficulties attributed to 'within-child' factors such as intelligence or attitude. In contrast, explanations for the West Indian children's difficulties are readily found in terms of 'within-child' factors such as attitude and IQ and also in factors connected with the home and family. The general pattern of the use of these causal attributions is the same for West Indian and white children but the West Indians are higher on all explanatory categories. Interestingly, this also holds good for the attribution of a child's difficulties to factors connected with teaching and the school. West Indian children are more likely than white children to have their difficulties attributed to the teachers and the school but this is still a small proportion in absolute terms.

49

5   Attitudes towards integration

The main concern of the present research project is with children placed in ordinary schools who have special needs – the one in five or one in six of the school population identified by Warnock – rather than with the fewer than one in fifty children placed in special schools or enjoying other sorts of special provision. However, it is clear that these are not two distinct groups of pupils: many children now in ordinary schools have problems very similar to the disabilities which have resulted in other children being educated in special schools. Whether or not a child is in special education depends not only on the level and type of his difficulties, but also on a number of other factors such as the availability and location of special school places and the facilities and approaches to special needs of ordinary schools.

In addition to the considerable overlap, currently existing, between the difficulties of children in special and normal provision there is a growing movement towards the integration of handicapped children in ordinary schools in so far as this is possible. This process, fairly widespread in western educational systems, has resulted in Public Law 94–142 in the United States and Section 10 of the 1976 Education Act in Britain, both of which made a very strong presumption that children should, whenever possible, be educated in ordinary schools. Section 10 was never implemented and has now been superseded but the current legislation, although not as strongly committed to integration as Section 10, requires that, subject to certain conditions, children with special needs should be placed in ordinary schools.

A recent NFER research project, after studying a number of integration programmes in England, concluded that:

> Special educational needs can be met in the ordinary school, and to a far greater extent than is currently the practice. There are many pupils in special schools at the moment who could be

educated satisfactorily in ordinary schools, given the requisite commitment and resources (Hegarty and Pocklington, 1981a).

This study emphasised the essential role of the teachers in such a process.

In the present research we investigated the experience which teachers in ordinary junior schools have had of handicapped pupils, how well they thought they had coped with these pupils in regular classes, and their attitudes towards the integration of pupils with various sorts of handicap in the regular classroom. Although most children previously categorised as handicapped are currently in special classes or special units, many junior-school teachers will have had experience of such pupils in an ordinary class since the majority of pupils in special education have arrived there via ordinary schools. In the case of ESN(M) and maladjusted pupils particularly, special education mainly comes about as a result of referral by a school, very often at junior level. Many teachers will have had pupils removed from their classes into special education, or pupils who may have been considered as candidates for special education but who, because of the non-availability of places, the unwillingness of their parents to have their children sent to special school or the determination of the school or teacher to keep the child in a particular classroom, have remained in an ordinary class. These examples refer mainly to children with learning difficulties or behavioural problems, but there are also instances where children with sensory or other physical difficulties are kept in an ordinary classroom and where children temporarily disabled by accident or illness have difficulties in many respects similar to those of some handicapped children.

These factors mean that the majority of junior school teachers have some experience of pupils who could be regarded as handicapped. When asked: 'Have you ever taught a child who could be regarded as handicapped in a regular class?', three-quarters of the teachers in our sample answered that they had. The percentage of teachers who claimed to have dealt with various categories of handicap in an ordinary class are presented in Table 5.1 alongside their estimates of how satisfactory they felt the arrangement was. (The percentages for how satisfactorily they coped with handicaps are based not on numbers of teachers but on the numbers of handicaps described. Many teachers discussed more than one child with particular sorts of difficulties with us and sometimes rated the different experiences differently.)

Table 5.1 Teachers' experience of children with handicaps

| | % of teachers with this experience | 'How well do you feel you coped?' | | | | |
		Very well %	Fairly well %	Mixed %	Not very well %	'Hopeless' %
ESN	44.4	20.5	27.8	12.1	34.8	4.8
Maladjusted	32.0	11.4	30.7	21.1	24.1	9.0
Hearing handicap	21.8	43.3	46.5	5.5	3.9	0.8
Visual handicap	6.9	54.8	29.0	—	12.9	3.2
Child in a wheelchair	5.2	59.1	22.7	9.1	9.1	—
Other restricted mobility	12.6	52.6	36.8	7.0	0.2	0.2
Other physical handicap	13.0	48.3	37.9	3.4	5.2	5.2

The first column in Table 5.1 shows the proportions of teachers in the sample who said they had had experience of at least one child with a handicap of some sort in their classrooms and, as might be expected, the largest proportion were ESN(M) children: 44 per cent of the teachers said that at some time they had had in their class a child with learning difficulties which they thought were severe enough to be classified as ESN(M). The next largest category was maladjustment: 32 per cent of the teachers said they had experienced a child in their class whose behavioural disturbances were severe enough for the child to be categorised as maladjusted. Among physical and sensory disabilities the largest category was hearing-impaired children: 21 per cent of the teachers said they had had experience of a hearing-impaired child in their class, while just under 7 per cent of the teachers had had experience of a visually handicapped child. Five per cent of the teachers had had experience of a child in a wheelchair in their class, 12 per cent had had experience of other children with mobility problems, and 13 per cent had had experience of children with other physical handicaps. In all, 28 per cent of the sample had had experience of some sort of physical handicap in their classroom.

It must be emphasised that these are teachers' own views on and definitions of handicap. The present study could not establish retrospectively the exact nature of the difficulties which the teachers were describing. Many of the pupils described to us were said by the teachers to have been categorised as ESN(M) or maladjusted, and many had come from or eventually gone to special education. Others, however, whose difficulties were thought by their teachers to be as severe as those of children classified as ESN(M) or maladjusted, had never been through an assessment procedure. Similarly, we do not know the extent of the hearing and visual handicaps or of the mobility and other problems. Moreover, some of the children with physical difficulties were suffering from temporary disabilities due to accidents or illness. Although the table cannot be taken as an indication of ordinary teachers' experience of pupils for whom special education would have been considered suitable, it does indicate teachers' own views of pupils whom they had had in their class and whom they would regard as falling into one of the statutory categories. Teachers' attitudes to such children as those classified ESN(M) and maladjusted will often be based on experience which the teachers believe they have had with such pupils in the ordinary classroom. Reactions to other sorts of difficulty, in particular visual handicaps or wheelchair-bound children, are much less likely to be based on personal experience.

The teachers were asked to describe how well they felt they had coped with the handicapped children whom they had had in their classes, and these results too are presented in Table 5.1. It is evident that the experience of having had sensorily handicapped and physically handicapped children in the classroom was generally considered far more satisfactory than the experience of having ESN(M) or mal-adjusted pupils there. In over 80 per cent of all the cases of physical or sensory problems the teachers said they had coped at least 'fairly well' and in over 40 per cent of all instances they felt they had coped 'very well'. In contrast, under half the teachers who had had experience of ESN(M) and maladjusted pupils felt that they had coped at least 'fairly well', and only 20 per cent and 11 per cent respectively felt that their experience of ESN(M) children and of maladjusted children had been very successful.

It is the most common categories of difficulties, those connected with learning and behaviour, that have given rise to the least satis-factory experiences of handicapped children in the ordinary class: these are also the difficulties which challenge the teacher's powers to teach and to keep control. Less common handicaps, which are also handicaps not centrally relevant to problems of classroom learning and adjustment, have given rise to the more satisfactory experiences.

After the teachers in the sample had been asked about their experiences of handicapped pupils in the ordinary classroom they were then asked about how they would react to having pupils with

Table 5.2 Teachers' opinions on integration of handicapped children in their own classrooms

		Enthus-iastic %	Fairly favourable %	Cautious %	Reluctant %	Refuse %	N
ESN(M)	No experience	6.8	17.9	26.8	36.6	11.9	235
	Experience	9.0	27.7	16.5	40.4	6.4	188
	All	7.8	22.2	22.2	38.3	9.5	423
Maladjusted	No experience	5.2	13.6	24.7	37.6	18.8	287
	Experience	5.9	21.5	22.2	37.0	13.3	135
	All	5.5	16.1	23.9	37.4	17.1	422
Part. hearing	No experience	20.3	41.8	18.5	16.1	3.3	330
	Experience	32.6	51.1	10.9	5.4	—	92
	All	23.0	43.8	16.8	13.7	2.6	422
Part. sighted	No experience	15.5	33.3	23.7	21.1	6.4	393
	Experience	41.4	27.6	17.2	10.3	3.4	29
	All	17.3	32.9	23.2	20.4	6.2	422
Child in a wheelchair	No experience	17.3	35.6	15.8	16.3	15.0	399
	Experience	31.8	36.4	9.1	13.6	9.1	22
	All	18.1	35.6	15.4	16.2	14.7	421
Other restricted mobility	No experience	21.4	45.8	15.7	14.1	3.0	369
	Experience	43.4	35.8	11.3	3.8	5.7	53
	All	24.2	44.5	15.2	12.8	3.3	422
Other physical handicap	No experience	22.6	40.3	18.3	15.0	3.8	367
	Experience	30.9	50.9	9.1	7.3	1.8	55
	All	23.7	41.7	17.1	14.0	3.6	422

these and other handicaps in their classes. For each handicap teachers were asked to say whether their response was best described as 'enthusiastic', 'fairly favourable', 'cautious', or 'reluctant', or whether they would refuse to have a child with this disability in their class. The results from these questions are presented in Table 5.2 both for the sample of teachers as a whole and separately for teachers with and without experience of the handicap in question. It should be noted that teachers were not responding to the principle of integration or to an ideally-run integration programme but to the idea that a handicapped child might be introduced into their classroom with no major changes in staffing or other provision to help them cope. A number of teachers indicated that they were more favourable to the principle of integration than was in fact borne out by their reactions to the idea of having a handicapped child in their own classroom. Many teachers pointed to the difficulties they were already experiencing, particularly when they were teaching large classes or pupils from socially dis-advantaged backgrounds. Other teachers said that, although they favoured the idea of handicapped children being in an ordinary school where possible, they felt that they personally lacked the training and expertise to deal with handicaps.

The teachers' reactions to various handicaps reinforced the conclusions which emerged from Table 5.1. Although there was much less experience of dealing with physically handicapped pupils in the ordinary class, there was also considerably more enthusiasm for it. About two-thirds of the teachers were at least 'fairly favourable' to the idea of having hearing-impaired pupils, pupils with restricted mobility, and pupils with other physical handicaps in their classes. Half the teachers were at least 'fairly favourable' to the idea of visually handicapped pupils and wheelchair-bound pupils in their classes. However, fewer than one teacher in three reacted favourably to the idea of ESN(M) pupils in a regular class, and only just over one in five reacted favourably to the idea of introducing maladjusted pupils.

It is important to be clear about the relationship between a teacher's experience of handicap and her willingness to have handicapped pupils in the classroom. As we have seen, the sorts of handicap that are most prevalent and most likely to have been experienced by ordinary teachers are the very ones that have given them the greatest dissatisfaction: it is exactly these ones, therefore, that they are least likely to welcome in the regular class. This, however, relates to teachers' comparative willingness to take different sorts of handicap, not to the impact of the experience of a particular handicap upon teachers' willingness to have children with these disabilities in future. This point emerges from a further consideration of Table 5.2, where reactions to various categories of handicapped pupils are presented separately for teachers who have had experience of such handicaps and teachers who have not. Uniformly throughout the table, teachers who have had experience of a given handicap are more willing to accept pupils with this difficulty in future than are teachers who have not. This applies not only to disabilities where overall willingness is fairly high, such as physical handicaps, but also to disabilities where teachers are on the whole much more reluctant, such as ESN(M) pupils and maladjusted pupils. The differences are the most extreme in the case of sensorily-handicapped pupils, where, in the case both of pupils with hearing impairments and of pupils with sight impairments, the difference between the percentage of teachers giving favourable reactions who have had experience and the percentage giving favourable reactions who have not is of the order of 20 per cent. In the case of children with wheelchairs the difference is about 15 per cent, and in the case of ESN(M) and maladjusted pupils about 10 per cent. Consistently, the experience of having taught children with any category of handicap is associated with the greater willingness to accept such children in one's own class, while inexperience of such children is associated with the lesser willingness. The difference in teacher reaction is greatest when the handicap under consideration is encountered relatively infrequently in the classroom: the more commonly-encountered handicaps elicit from experienced and non-experienced teachers less sharply different reactions. A further point of interest arising from Table 5.2 is that teachers' reactions to the less frequent handicaps fall within the bands of a relatively favourable overall response, while reactions to handicaps more often met with in the classroom express rather more reluctance.

We have been careful to talk of an association rather than of any necessary causal factors in this observed correlation. It may be that experience predisposes people towards a more favourable attitude: the relatively successful experiences described by some teachers would support this view. It may also be, however, that only where teachers are particularly favourably disposed towards integration, or only where conditions are particularly favourable, is the experience of certain sorts of handicaps in the classroom likely to have arisen. It should also be noted that the association between experience of handicapped pupils and a welcoming attitude towards them is an imperfect one; there are examples of teachers who have had handicapped pupils in their class who would be reluctant to repeat the experience or even in some cases say that they would refuse to do so.

The general pattern of association discussed above accords with the results of other studies, such as the recent NFER integration study (Hegarty and Pocklington, 1981a), which have concluded that teachers' initial reluctance and uncertainty about integration programmes have generally given way to a more positive response following experience of the operation of the programme.

A hypothesis suggested by the results of the pilot study was that, while class teachers would be relatively favourable towards the integration of handicapped pupils, head teachers would be much more cautious and would be more likely to emphasise the practical difficulties and the limitations of available resources and expertise

(Moses, 1982). However, when the results of questions asked of head teachers about children with various handicaps attending their school are compared with the same questions asked of class teachers, this hypothesis is not confirmed. In Table 5.3 the only consistent difference which emerges between teachers and heads is a tendency for heads to answer the questions more decisively. For all categories of handicap heads are less likely than teachers to use the middle category 'cautious', and for almost all the questions they are more likely to use the two extreme categories of 'enthusiastic' and 'refuse'. The general direction of their responses, however, does not differ in a consistent fashion from that of the teachers. Like teachers, heads are more favourably disposed to the integration of sensorily and physically handicapped children in their schools than they are to ESN(M) and maladjusted pupils. For particular categories of physical and sensory disability the differences between the heads and the teachers are not very great and do not follow any consistent pattern. Heads are more favourable than teachers to the integration of ESN(M) pupils and slightly more favourable to the integration of maladjusted pupils.

Table 5.3 *Class teachers' and Head teachers' attitudes towards various handicaps in the ordinary classroom*

		Enthus- iastic %	Fairly favourable %	Cautious %	Reluctant %	Refuse %	N
ESN(M)	Teachers	7.8	22.2	22.2	38.3	9.5	423
	Heads	16.4	23.0	16.4	29.5	14.8	61
Maladjusted	Teachers	5.5	16.1	23.9	37.4	17.1	422
	Heads	3.4	22.0	22.0	28.8	23.7	59
Part. hearing	Teachers	23.0	43.8	16.8	13.7	2.6	422
	Heads	30.0	31.7	11.7	23.3	3.3	60
Part. sighted	Teachers	17.3	32.9	23.2	20.4	6.2	422
	Heads	25.0	31.7	13.3	21.7	8.3	60
Child in a wheelchair	Teachers	18.1	35.6	15.4	16.2	14.7	421
	Heads	21.7	30.0	10.0	13.3	25.0	60
Other restricted mobility	Teachers	24.2	44.5	15.2	12.8	3.3	422
	Heads	30.5	33.9	11.9	15.3	8.5	59
Other physical handicap	Teachers	23.7	41.7	17.1	14.0	3.6	422
	Heads	35.0	35.0	11.7	15.0	3.3	60

A different perspective on these attitudinal data is provided by the assessments teachers made of their pupils in their class. The teacher, having described a child as presenting special educational needs, was then asked what she thought was the appropriate educational placement for the child. The great majority of these children were believed by the teachers to be appropriately placed in ordinary class-rooms, the considerable difficulties which they presented there not-withstanding. Just under one in twenty of the pupils with special needs were thought by their teachers to need education in a special school, and about twice this number of the children discussed were thought by their teachers likely to benefit from a special class within the ordinary school. These figures represent 0.9 per cent and 1.6 per cent of all pupils in the classes studied. Problems of learning and behaviour, which emerged in the attitudinal data as matters of prime concern, also dominate the teachers' considerations of a special school placement. There was only one child in all the 428 classrooms visited who was thought by his teacher to need to attend a special school and who had neither learning nor behaviour problems.

The teacher responses in our sample to handicapped junior-age children are similar to those reported by Chazan *et al.*, in connection with the integration of nursery-age children:

> D's teacher came nearest to revealing why this group of children [those with physical handicaps] can be coped with so well. None of them suffered from mental retardation or, as yet, from emotional upsets. When a teacher finds a child rewarding to teach she is prepared to accept his physical difficulties (Chazan *et al.*, 1980, p. 176).

Teachers' relatively favourable responses to physical and sensory handicaps are not necessarily based on a realistic assessment of what the regular classroom can offer to a child with these sorts of difficulty. We must be careful not to take it for granted that integration is always the best solution for a child or to assume that a positive attitude towards integration is always the most desirable response from a teacher, particularly given the difficult physical and social contexts within which some of the teachers in the sample worked. Nevertheless, there is little doubt that there are children in special schools who could be successfully integrated into ordinary schools and classrooms, and the classroom teachers' response to sensorily and physically handicapped pupils is encouraging to those wishing to see more integration of children with these handicaps. However, any extensive integration of children currently categorised as handicapped would have to involve ESN(M) and maladjusted pupils, towards whom teachers' responses are least enthusiastic. It is worth noting that, despite the association between a teacher having had experience of a particular handicap and her subsequent willingness to accept that handicap in the ordinary class, over one-third of the teachers who had had experience of ESN(M) and maladjusted pupils expressed reluctance to accept them a second time. These are also the children whose difficulties are most clearly bound up with the requirements which the educational system imposes on pupils rather than with difficulties which are only incidentally related to education.

6 Reading achievement and teacher assessment

Introduction

The analysis conducted in Chapter 3 was concerned with data derived from the descriptions teachers gave of their pupils. The discussion of the incidence of special needs of various kinds, of the overlap between types of special educational need, of variations across schools and classes and of differences in the incidence of special needs among different groups of pupils were all based on the teachers' descriptions without reference to any other sources of information about the children. For example, most teachers used the term 'poor reader' in discussing some of the children in their class, and, whether or not a teacher had used this term, the expression was introduced by the researchers at a later stage when teachers were prompted about different sorts of educational difficulties children might have. From the way in which teachers introduced this phrase (or something very similar) spontaneously and from the way in which they immediately accepted it as meaningful when it was introduced by the researchers, it is clear that this is a very common way of thinking about children's learning difficulties and a type of classification which is frequently applied to pupils. More than seven out of ten of the pupils described by their teachers as having special educational needs were described as poor readers, and in most cases this was a concept introduced by the teacher rather than prompted by the researchers. Although the concept is obviously a central one for teachers, from the analysis so far presented it is not clear exactly how they use it. In particular, it is unclear what level of reading difficulty teachers associate with the notion of being a poor reader. It was extremely unusual in the interviews for teachers to ask the researchers what level of reading difficulty they meant by the term 'poor readers', and it was fairly unusual for teachers to discuss pupils in terms of explicit criteria for reading achievement.

The same absence of definition is found in the evaluative terms used in other areas of special educational needs. Teachers were not asked to describe, nor did they generally volunteer, exact descriptions of degrees of behavioural disturbance, discipline problems and so on. In the area of reading performance, however, it is relatively straightforward to get measures of children's reading achievements and difficulties which are independent of the teachers' assessments and views of the child. In the present study, reading test scores, typically in the form of reading ages, were obtained whenever possible for children whom their teachers regarded as having any sort of special educational need. As will be shown in the discussion of testing in schools in Chapter 7, most primary school teachers use reading tests with their pupils. These results are, of course, derived from a variety of different tests in different classrooms, have been administered at varying lengths of time before the point at which the information was collected and have been administered in different settings and, possibly, with varying degrees of competence. Nevertheless, they provide a rough and ready indication of the levels of reading achievement of pupils described by their teachers as being poor readers.

In addition to data collected from the teachers, the SPAR reading test was administered by the research team in thirty-four second-year classes in two of the local authorities in the study. This provides a measure of children's reading achievements in a systematic fashion independent of teacher assessments and teacher-administered tests.

Using these sources of data it is possible to describe reading achievements of pupils regarded by their teachers as being poor readers. There are a number of questions to which this analysis addresses itself. In the first place, it is possible to give a straightforward description of the degree of reading difficulty experienced by pupils described as poor readers and to consider the extent of the variation in the difficulties of different pupils within this category. It is also possible to approach the question slightly differently and to consider the likelihood of a child with a particular level of reading difficulties being described as a poor reader. A comparison of such levels with teachers' assessments of reading difficulties makes it possible to root the latter more concretely in the difficulties of pupils. Teachers in the study were not asked what they meant by 'poor reader' but it is possible to infer something about teachers' concepts from the test scores of the pupils. This second kind of question treats teacher assessments in a rather different fashion from the way in which they have been regarded so far in the analysis. So far teacher assessments of pupils have been taken, in a sense, at 'face value', but comparison of these test results with teacher assessments enables the assessments as well as the scores to be regarded as, at least potentially, problematic. Variations in the relationship between test scores and teacher assessments can themselves be considered and can be related to other characteristics of the child, the class and the teacher.

It is important to be clear what is being attempted here. It is not being suggested that test scores provide an objective once-and-for-all description of a child's reading achievements against which fallible teacher assessments can be judged. Where there is an apparent discrepancy between the teacher's description and the child's test performance (for example, a child described as a poor reader who performs at an average or better level in the test, or a child not so described who performs very poorly), it cannot be assumed that the test provides an accurate measure and the teacher is mistaken. All tests have an element of unreliability, and a short group reading test is only a limited measure of children's reading performance. Consequently, apparent discrepancies between test scores and teacher assessments are regarded as something to be further investigated rather than as an indication either of inaccurate teacher assessments or of unsatisfactory test results. This investigation will proceed by introducing further variables into the analysis so that possible explanations for differences can be evaluated. If apparent discrepancies can be shown to be associated with the operation of other variables in a consistent fashion which accords with the explanations being considered, such explanations will be thereby supported.

Reading test scores and teacher nominations

A description of the level of reading difficulties experienced by pupils regarded by their teachers as poor readers is represented in Table 6.1, which shows reading test results obtained from the schools' or the teachers' records. As was pointed out above, these data must be treated tentatively. Results from a whole variety of different types of tests administered in different circumstances are included in the table. Sometimes the tests had been administered recently but often they were a term or more out of date. They are used here to present a

Table 6.1 Reading ages of nominated poor readers by sex and age

		All pupils	Sex Boys	Girls	Age 1st years	2nd years	3rd years	4th years
RA 2 years or more behind	N	630	422	208	106	134	203	187
CA[1]	%	45.8	46.9	43.5	29.1	35.0	57.3	67.8
RA 1 to 2 years behind	N	425	270	155	132	148	95	50
CA	%	30.9	30.0	32.4	36.3	38.6	26.3	18.1
RA less than 1 year behind	N	322	207	115	126	101	56	49
CA	%	23.4	23.0	24.1	34.6	26.4	15.8	17.8
N =		1377	899	478	364	383	354	276

[1] RA = Reading Age; CA = Chronological Age.
The figures for pupils two or more years behind include some children who fail to register a reading age on the tests.

very rough overview of the level of difficulties experienced by those nominated poor readers for whom these results are available.

The first column of Table 6.1 shows the level of reading achievement of poor readers as a whole: 45.8 per cent of pupils described as poor readers are two years or more behind their chronological age on standardised tests of reading achievement, while a further 30.9 per cent are between one and two years behind. In all, over three-quarters of these children are a year or more behind their chronological age. The remaining 23.4 per cent of the poor readers, by contrast, are less than a year behind their chronological age on the school's reading test records or, in a few cases, are not behind at all.

Table 6.1 also provides comparisons between boys and girls and between different year groups in terms of the reading test scores among nominated poor readers. The first comparison reveals only small differences between the groups. Boys nominated as poor readers are slightly more likely than girls nominated as poor readers to be two years or more behind their chronological age. Much more dramatic differences emerge when comparisons are made between the four different year groups within the junior school. Among the first-years in the sample 29.1 per cent of the poor readers are two years or more behind, and over a third, 34.6 per cent, are less than a year behind their chronological age. Among the second-years the proportion two years or more behind has risen to 35.0 per cent and among the third-years to 57.3 per cent. Among the fourth-years in the sample 67.8 per cent are two years or more behind, more than double the proportion of first-year poor readers. Conversely, the proportion of poor readers who are less than a year behind among the fourth-years is about half the proportion of first-year pupils.

As has been stressed, these figures must be treated cautiously and in part reflect characteristics of the tests being used and the circumstances in which they are used. For example, although the first-years are on average less far behind their chronological age, a much higher proportion of them do not perform well enough on reading tests to be given a reading age at all. Such children have been described as being two years or more behind. This, however, reinforces the suggestion that at the early stages pupils may be regarded as poor readers when their difficulties relative to the rest of the class are less severe than those of pupils so regarded at a later stage in the junior school. The same point has already been considered in Chapter 3 where it was shown that, as would be expected from the above results, a higher proportion of the younger than of the older age groups are identified by their teachers as having special educational needs. These results tend to confirm the conclusion suggested in Chapter 3, that teachers do not judge special educational needs simply in terms of pupils' relative positions in the class and consequently do not describe a more or less fixed proportion of their class as having special educational needs. Among the younger pupils, where overall level of achievement is of course lower, a higher proportion of the children are described as having difficulties. Children who, relative to their peers, must be performing as poorly as the younger children who are described as having learning problems are, because of their higher level of achievement in absolute terms, not described as having such learning difficulties when they are in third- and fourth-year classes.

The results in Table 6.1 refer only to characteristics of pupils described as poor readers and do not enable comparisons to be made between such pupils and other children in the class who have not been identified by their teachers as having reading difficulties. In particular, it is not possible, from the results in Table 6.1, to describe the likelihood that a child with a particular level of difficulty will be identified as being a poor reader. Such an analysis can be conducted, however, using the results of reading tests administered in thirty-four second-year classes. The SPAR reading test, a group reading test, was administered to 751 pupils in these classes. The SPAR test is particularly suitable to the second-year classes as it give results which can be converted to reading ages of 5.9 to 10.8 (although these are reading ages they are expressed in years and tenths rather than in years and months).

Table 6.2 SPAR reading test and teacher-nominated 'poor readers' for 751 second-year pupils

Reading age		All pupils	Poor readers	% nominated
2 years or more behind	N	39	29	74.4
	%	5.2	35.4	
1 year and less than	N	111	35	31.5
2 years behind	%	14.8	42.7	
Behind but less than	N	204	17	8.3
1 year behind	%	27.2	20.7	
Not behind chronological	N	397	1	0.3
age	%	52.9	1.2	
Total =		751	82	10.9

In Table 6.2 the test scores of the second-year pupils are presented. They have been broken down into four groups: children who are two years or more behind their chronological age in the reading test score, children who are a year behind but less than two years behind, children who are behind their chronological age but less than a year behind and children who are not behind their chronological age. The results for all the second-years are presented in the first column of the table. Approximately half the pupils are behind their chronological age to some extent, as must necessarily be the case when test scores are standardised for age. Just over 5 per cent of pupils are two years or more behind and 14.8 per cent are a year behind but less than two years behind. The second column of Table 6.2 presents these figures for children described by their teachers as poor readers. Their distribution of reading scores is very similar to that of the total sample of nominated poor readers in the second-year age group presented in Table 6.1. Rather more than a third of the poor readers in Table 6.2 are two years or more behind their chronological ages, and nearly four in five of the children described as poor readers are a year or more behind. In contrast, just over one in five of the children described as poor readers are less than a year behind their chronological age.

In the third column of Table 6.2 these figures are expressed as percentages of children at particular levels of test scores who are identified by their teachers as poor readers: 74.4 per cent of children two years or more behind are identified as poor readers, 31.5 per cent of children between a year and two years behind are identified as poor readers and 8.3 per cent of children behind their chronological age but less than a year behind are regarded as poor readers by their teachers.

In the sample as a whole, just over 45 per cent of poor readers had reading ages two years or more behind, and more than three-quarters were a year or more behind. Among the second-year pupils studied in more detail, a child two years or more behind stood a three out of four chance of being regarded by his teacher as a poor reader, while a child between one and two years behind stood less than a one-in-three chance of being so regarded.

Reading ages, teacher nominations and other pupil characteristics

As was stated earlier, when apparent mismatches occur between teacher assessments of children and the results of standardised tests, whether the assessments have been made by different teachers who have differing views of children at apparently identical levels of achievement or by individual teachers who appear to be inconsistent in their application of the notion of poor reader to pupils in their class, the mismatches are not amenable to simple interpretation. It may be that teachers' assessments are influenced by considerations other than the child's actual level of achievement as measured by the test, or it may be that the test has failed to give a proper reflection of a child's achievements. This second source of explanation is particularly applicable where a child has performed less well on the test than the teacher assessment would imply, as there are a number of possible explanations for such variation. Where a child has performed well on a test there is less reason to doubt that he is at least capable of performing at this level.

In order to examine the possible explanations of variations between teacher assessments and test performance, a number of other characteristics of the pupils, not apparently having an intrinsic relationship either to teachers' assessments of reading difficulties or to

Table 6.3 Sex differences among teacher-nominated poor readers: 751 second-year pupils

Reading age		All	Boys Poor readers	% nominated	All	Girls Poor readers	% nominated
2 years or	N	26	18	69.2	13	11	84.6
more behind	%	6.7	30.5		3.6	47.8	
1 year and							
less than 2	N	68	27	39.7	43	8	18.6
years behind	%	17.6	45.8		11.8	34.9	
Behind but							
less than	N	109	14	12.8	95	3	3.2
1 year behind	%	28.2	23.7		26.1	13.0	
Not behind							
chronological	N	184	—	—	213	1	0.5
age	%	47.5	—		58.5	4.3	
Total =		387	59	15.2	364	23	6.3

test performance, will be introduced into the analysis.

In Table 6.3 the relationship between pupils' measured reading age and teacher nominations of poor readers is shown separately for boys and girls in thirty-four second-year classes. It is immediately apparent that boys outnumber girls among those who are furthest behind in their reading and also among those who are regarded by their teachers as poor readers. The percentage of boys two years or more behind their chronological age is almost double the percentage of girls falling into this group, and the percentage of boys at least a year but less than two years behind is half as great again as the percentage of girls. Paralleling this result is the fact that teachers regard 6.3 per cent of girls in their classes as poor readers and 15.2 per cent of the boys. These results are in line with those from a number of previous studies. For example, in the National Children's Bureau research presented in the report of the Plowden Committee girls performed more successfully than boys on reading tests and were also more highly assessed on reading skills by their teachers: nearly twice as many boys as girls were described as 'poor readers' or worse by their teachers (DES, 1967, p. 433). Similar results are also reported in *The Home and the School* (Douglas, 1967, pp. 98–104).

The suggestion has sometimes been made, however, that the superior performance of girls in tests of reading abilities does not entirely account for their teachers' higher ratings of girls. This point is made in Douglas's study, which looks at both test results and teacher assessments, and also in the research of Arnold, who suggests that primary-school teachers are found to overestimate the reading skills of girls and underestimate those of boys when assessments are compared with test performance (Arnold, 1977). Table 6.3 gives support to the view that teachers may overestimate girls relative to boys or, put the other way round, that teachers may sometimes fail to recognise the reading difficulties experienced by girls in their class. It is clear from Table 6.3 that the smaller proportion of girls regarded as poor readers cannot be entirely accounted for in terms of their superior achievements. Of the 94 boys who are at least a year behind their chronological age 45, or 47.9 per cent, are described as poor readers, while of the 56 girls who are at least a year behind only 19, or 30.6 per cent, are so regarded. This gender difference in teacher nominations does not hold at all levels of reading difficulty. Among the poorest readers, those two years or more behind, girls are rather more likely to be nominated as poor readers. Among pupils at least a year but not two years behind, boys are more than twice as likely to be regarded as poor readers by their teachers and boys who are behind their chrono-logical age by less than one year are four times as likely to be nominated by their teachers as having reading difficulties.

Previous discussions of the relationship between teacher views of their pupils and the pupils' actual performance have tended to con-centrate on the possible advantages accruing to children who are favourably regarded by their teachers and the disadvantages of being less well regarded. Concern with the effect of teacher expectancies and with 'self-fulfilling prophecies' has led researchers to concentrate on the positive aspects of being favourably regarded by teachers and the possible unfairness this involves to other children in the class. Nevertheless, there is little solid evidence for such processes (see Boydell, 1978, chapter 6, and Croll, 1981, for discussions of this research) and it is, on the face of it, at least as plausible that a child may be disadvantaged by not having his or her difficulties recognised as that such a recognition will become self-fulfilling. The question of the consequences for children of being assessed as having learning difficulties will be considered in Chapter 8.

Another factor which may be relevant to the relationship between teacher assessment and test scores, although it is not intrinsically related to either, is a child's position as one of the older or younger members of a class. Within a single-age-group junior class the age range of the children can be almost a year. In children of this age a year represents a considerable increase in intellectual development even where it does not (and sometimes it will) reflect differences in length of formal schooling. In the pilot study for the present research (Moses, 1982) it was found that children whose low scores on standardised tests surprised their teachers were disproportionately likely to be the oldest children in the class. It was suggested that, while standardised tests correct the effects of the children's age, the day-by-day process of assessing work in the classroom does not take account of this factor. Consequently the older children in a class are likely to be more favourably perceived by their teachers than their performance on a standardised test would justify, and younger children will be less favourably perceived.

This suggestion is borne out by the analyses presented in Table 6.4. Pupils have been divided into three groups according to their month of birth: the oldest children in the class, born between September and December, a middle group of children born between January and April and the youngest children, born between May and August. As the first column of Table 6.4 shows, children's births are relatively evenly spread over these three periods of time. In the second block of Table 6.4 pupils described by their teachers as poor readers whose test results suggested that they were less than a year behind their chronological age are identified by their months of birth. Two-thirds of these pupils are among the youngest children in the class, and only one child comes from the oldest group. The opposite case, namely those children who are not described as poor readers but who do have poor scores on the tests of achievement, shows a reverse pattern. Of pupils not described as poor readers who are two years or more

Table 6.4 *Birth dates and teacher nominations of poor readers: second-year pupils*

Birth dates	All pupils		Nominated poor readers < 1 year behind		Not nominated poor readers 2 years behind		1–2 years behind	
	N	%	N	%	N	%	N	%
Sept–Dec	234	30.7	1	5.6	6	60.0	34	44.7
January–April	260	34.1	5	27.8	3	30.0	31	40.8
May–August	268	35.2	12	66.7	1	10.0	11	14.5
Total =	762	100	18	100	10	100	76	100

behind, six out of ten are from the oldest group in the class and only one out of ten is from the youngest. Among pupils between one and two years behind the differences are not quite so dramatic but are still considerable: more than three times as many children come from the oldest group as come from the youngest group.

These results confirm the hypothesis suggested by the pilot study that in making assessments teachers will tend not to correct for the effects of different ages of children in their classes. The point will be pursued, together with the related question of how test results and other records of pupils' achievement are kept, in Chapter 7.

Another characteristic of pupils potentially relevant to the relationship between teacher assessment and test scores is whether or not the pupils are regarded by their teachers as having behaviour problems. In Chapter 3 it was shown that teachers' views of pupils as having learning difficulties and as having behaviour problems overlap considerably. Two-thirds of the children described by their teachers as having behavioural difficulties were also described as having learning problems; these pupils make up over a third of the total pupils with learning difficulties. This association between learning and behaviour problems is a feature of other work in this area such as the Isle of Wight study (Rutter, Tizard and Whitmore, 1970) and the National Children's Bureau study (Pringle et al., 1966). A number of recent articles have attempted to disentangle the causal relationships between behavioural and learning difficulties (Stott,1982, Youngman, 1982 and Kash and Moore, 1982). In Stott's view the causal explanation which best fits the data from his research suggests that, in general, it is behavioural difficulties that inhibit learning and so cause learning difficulties: behavioural difficulties do not usually arise as a result of frustration or other response to learning failure. A doubtful point in these researches, which is also shared by the present analysis, is that the measurement of behavioural characteristics depends for the most part on the ratings made by teachers. In the analysis being presented here, a teacher's nomination of a child as a behavioural problem has a rather different status as a pupil characteristic from sex or month of birth or score on a reading test. These latter variables have no intrinsic relationship to the views teachers take of their pupils' reading problems; but nominations of behaviour problems and of poor readers were elicited from the teachers in the same way by the researchers.

Table 6.5 shows a strong association both between children being

Table 6.5 *Behaviour problems and teacher assessment of reading problems: second-year pupils*

Reading ages		Nominated behaviour problems			Not behaviour problems		
		Total	Nominated poor readers		Total	Nominated poor readers	
			N	%		N	%
2 years or	N	13	12	92.3	26	17	65.4
more behind	%	19.4			3.8		
1 year and less than 2 years	N	17	12	70.6	94	23	24.5
behind	%	25.4			13.7		
Less than 1 year	N	21	5	17.2	183	12	6.6
behind	%	31.3			26.8		
Not behind chronological	N	16	0	0	381	1	0.3
age	%	23.9			55.7		
Total =		67	29	43.3	684	53	7.7

nominated as behaviour problems and their being nominated as poor readers and also between being nominated as behaviour problems and poor test performance. Of the sixty-seven children regarded by their teachers as behaviour problems 43.3 per cent are also described as poor readers, while of the 684 not regarded as behaviour problems 7.7 per cent are nominated as poor readers. Children nominated as behaviour problems are also far more likely than other children to be behind on reading tests: 19.4 per cent are two years or more behind compared with 3.8 per cent of the other pupils, and 25.4 per cent are between one and two years behind compared with 13.7 per cent of the other pupils. The strong association between descriptions of a child as a behaviour problem and as a poor reader is not, however, accounted for by the poorer reading achievements of these children. At particular levels of reading difficulty children described as behaviour problems are very much more likely than other children to be nominated as poor readers. Of the behaviour problems who are two years or more behind 92.3 per cent are described as poor readers, while of the other children two years or more behind 65.4 per cent are so described. Among nominated behaviour problems between one and two years behind, 70.6 per cent are also described as poor readers compared with 24.5 per cent of other children, and among the children behind their chronological age by less than one year, 17.2 per cent of the behaviour problems are described as poor readers compared with 6.6 per cent of those not described as behaviour problems. It seems clear that there is an association between teachers' descriptions of children as poor readers and descriptions of them as behaviour problems independent of the fact that children with behavioural difficulties also have poorer reading skills.

Overall class performance and teacher assessment of poor readers

The variables considered so far as offering possible explanations for patterns of variation in the relationship of teacher assessments to test scores have been derived from characteristics of individual pupils. A further possibility is that characteristics of the class as a whole may influence the way in which teachers view children's difficulties, and one particular characteristic of this kind is the average class reading achievement measured by the median class score (that is, the score of the boy or girl who is exactly half-way on a ranking order of reading achievement).

It is clear that identifying children with reading difficulties, particularly when reading skills are still developing, inevitably involves an element of comparison with the reading skills of other children. It seems likely that teachers may judge the reading performance of children in their class not with respect to the performance of children in general, but with respect to the overall level of class performance. Occasionally in the interviews with teachers this was made explicit, and the teacher would describe a child as having reading problems in comparison with the present class although the child's difficulties would not have made him a poor reader in other classes of which the teachers had had experience. It seems possible, therefore, that children in classes where the overall level of performance is high may be identified as poor readers, even though the levels of reading achievement are similar to those of children not identified as poor readers in classes where the overall level of achievement is low.

In Table 6.6 the thirty-four second-year classes in which tests were conducted have been divided into four groups on the basis of the median level of reading achievement in the class. The first comparison among these four groups is concerned with all the pupils in the classes who are at least a year behind their chronological age but

Table 6.6 Overall class performance and teacher assessments of reading in thirty-four second-year classes

Median class reading score	No. of classes	No. of pupils at least 1 year and less than 2 years behind	% nominated 'poor readers'	No. of pupils at least 2 years behind	% nominated 'poor readers'
Highest group*	8	18	50.0	3	66.7
Second highest group	10	23	43.5	2	100
Second lowest group	8	28	32.1	11	81.8
Lowest group	8	42	19.0	23	69.6

* The highest group had median reading ages six months or more ahead of chronological age, the second highest had medians above chronological age by less than six months, the second lowest had median scores at chronological age or behind by less than six months and the lowest had medians six months or more behind.

are not two years or more behind. There is a clear and consistent relationship between the overall level of class achievement and the likelihood that these children will be identified by their teachers as poor readers. In the highest achieving group of classes 50.0 per cent of the pupils between one and two years behind are described by their teachers as poor readers; in the next highest achieving group of classes 43.5 per cent are identified; in the next highest group 32.1 per cent are identified, and in the lowest achieving group of classes only 19.0 per cent of pupils between one and two years behind their chronological age were described as poor readers by their teachers.

The second comparison is concerned with the poorest achieving pupils, those who are two years or more behind their chronological age in their reading test score. This comparison must be treated tentatively, as in the two highest achieving groups of classes the numbers of such children are very small. For this group of pupils there is no consistent pattern of decline in the likelihood of being identified as poor readers as the overall level of class achievement declines. Two-thirds of the pupils in this group in both the highest and lowest achieving group of classes are identified as poor readers, while all the pupils in the second highest achieving group and 81.8 per cent of those in the third highest group are described as poor readers. These

73

figures offer some support to the conclusion of Moses (Moses, 1980) that, while children with the lowest levels of reading achievement are identified as poor readers whatever the overall level of class performance, the identification of children with less severe reading difficulties will be influenced by the general level of achievement in the class. However, it must be emphasised again that numbers of children two years or more behind in the higher achieving classes are too small for any firm conclusions to be drawn, and there is a small decrease in the likelihood of identification of these pupils between the third highest and the lowest group of classes.

Overview: reading achievement and teacher assessments

It is clear that, in assessing pupils as poor readers, teachers do not in general apply a simple cut-off point in terms of test score or a fixed number of years and months behind a child's chronological age. Nevertheless there is, as would be expected, a strong relationship between teacher assessment and children's test performances. Over three-quarters of the children in the sample who were described as poor readers are at least a year behind and nearly a half are two years behind their chronological ages on school-administered reading tests. Among second-year pupils three-quarters of those two years or more behind were described as poor readers, as were nearly a third of pupils at least one year but less than two years behind. Very few pupils less than a year behind were described as poor readers. These results suggest a flexibility among teachers in the assessments they make, but they also suggest that different teachers may be applying different criteria to establish the level of achievement that is to be regarded as reading difficulty and may be applying the notions of poor reader differentially to different groups of children.

The systematic patterns of difference in the way different teachers apply the notion of poor reader show the influence both of absolute levels of reading achievement and of the ways that judgments are made relative to the performance of others. The results for the whole junior-age sample show that a higher proportion of first-year than of fourth-year pupils are judged to be poor readers. At these younger age ranges a difficulty relative to other pupils is far more likely to be identified as poor reading than the same relative level of difficulty among the older pupils. Nevertheless, teachers cannot simply apply an absolute criterion to all pupils: compared with the teacher, for example, most junior school pupils are poor readers. The influence of judgments made relative to others is shown when teacher assessments are compared across classes at different average levels of achievement. At identical levels of difficulty in terms of national norms a child is much more likely to be identified as a poor reader if he is in a high-achieving class than if the average class reading performance is poor.

These influences on teacher assessments appear in the way that judgments are made of all pupils in a particular class. The characteristics of individual pupils, however, also seem to influence teacher assessments. From the data presented above it seems that sex, age within the class and the fact of being perceived as a behaviour problem are all related to the assessments teachers make. At particular levels of reading achievement, as measured by reading tests, boys are more likely than girls to be described as poor readers, younger children are more likely than older children and children described as behaviour problems are more likely than other pupils to be nominated. As was pointed out at the beginning of this chapter, apparent variations and inconsistencies in the relationships between teacher assessments and test scores are not susceptible to simple explanations. In particular, it cannot be assumed that such discrepancies reflect errors in teacher assessments. However, by looking at systematic patterns in such variations it is possible to assess possible explanatory factors. Various possible factors have been considered above. These sorts of explanation clearly relate to variations in teacher assessments rather than in test scores, although in later chapters test scores themselves will be the subject of this kind of analysis. It is reasonable to expect that the relative ages of pupils within a class, overall class achievement, pupil behaviour and, in the context of other studies, sex, will influence the views teachers have of their pupils. It is less reasonable to assume that girls, older children and children without behaviour problems under-achieve on tests relative to their all-round class performance. Explanations in terms of influence on teacher assessments are compatible with the data and fit in with what is known from other studies of the ways in which assessments are made.

7 Testing and assessment in junior classrooms

All teachers are continuously making assessments of the children in their classes. These assessments can be based on a number of criteria involving quite different processes. An assessment can be based solely on the overall impression a child makes in the classroom; it can be based on detailed accounts of the work a child does day by day; or it could be based on the results of standardised tests. Usually assessments include all three elements but the emphasis can vary considerably. In earlier chapters it was shown that teachers' assessments of children's abilities are based largely upon the teacher's estimate of how well a child can read and this in turn is affected by a number of factors that include sex, behaviour and the overall level of the class as well as the individual child's performance.

Although the teacher's observations of pupils and records of classroom work are of great importance, standardised tests also have a role to play. Test scores can give the teacher additional information about a child that may be illuminating. In large classes, where teachers inevitably have only a limited amount of time to spend with each child, some children may develop strategies of classroom behaviour that may make it very difficult for the teacher to identify the child who has a learning difficulty and needs help. Conversely, a test score may indicate that a child has abilities that have not previously been recognised. A child's test score can cause a teacher to take another look at a child and possibly modify her opinion of his or her capabilities. The value of standardised testing procedures was recognised in the Warnock Report: 'We therefore recommend that local education authorities should operate procedures for monitoring whole age groups of children at least three or four times during their school life' (p.57). The majority of LEAs do operate such a system, though the extent and type of testing varies.

Table 7.1 Testing in junior classrooms

	N	%
Classrooms where reading tests are used for whole class	388	90.7
Classrooms where reading tests are used for at least some of the children	392	91.6
Classrooms where other achievement tests are used	289	67.5
Classrooms where reasoning tests (verbal reasoning, non-verbal reasoning) are used	115	26.9
Classrooms where no tests are used	26	6.1
Classrooms where testing includes maths	260	60.8
Classrooms where children with learning difficulties are tested more frequently than others	137	32.0
Total number of classrooms	428	100.0

In addition to the LEA initiatives the majority of schools also run their own testing programmes. During the years spent in the primary school most children will, at some time, be required to take one or more standardised tests both as part of the ordinary business of the classroom and also because it forms part of the policy of the local education authority.

The most striking findings presented in Table 7.1 are the very widespread use of tests in junior schools and the frequency with which reading tests in particular are used. Teachers in over 91 per cent of classrooms used a reading test for at least some children, and very slightly fewer, still over 90 per cent, tested the reading skills of the whole class at least once during the school year. This emphasis on the testing of reading is not surprising given the central position of reading in the primary school. Nevertheless, other types of test were also widely used. Children in over 67 per cent of classrooms were given a variety of achievement tests, and in over 60 per cent of classrooms tests of mathematic skill were included. Far fewer children were in classrooms where either verbal reasoning or non-verbal reasoning tests were used. A substantial amount of this type of testing was conducted by the schools at the request of the local authority rather than as an activity originating from within the individual school. Only 16.8 per cent of schools used reasoning tests when they did not form part of the testing programme of the authority. The skills that reasoning tests measure, particularly non-verbal tests, are less obvious to teachers than reading and may be regarded by them as being of less interest. However, it is just this type of test that may indicate to a teacher that a child is capable of thinking in a way that he has not displayed in the classroom. In particular, a non-verbal reasoning test result may tell the teacher that a child who is a poor reader is not necessarily a slow learner in other respects. Although it is true that some testing in schools is the result of LEA policy it would be quite mistaken to suppose that testing programmes are inflicted upon unwilling schools. Much of the testing carried out in junior classrooms is part of the internal policy of the school and part of regular classroom activity.

Testing and LEA policy

Six out of the ten authorities in this study had a policy on the testing of junior school age children which involved the administration of standardised tests to whole year groups of children.

Reading was the skill most frequently tested by both schools and LEAs. And all the authorities that conducted any form of testing used reading tests. In addition to reading, three authorities used verbal reasoning tests and two maths tests and one a more general language test. Typically, the tests were administered by the teachers and often marked by them also, but the results were analysed outside the school. There was considerable uniformity about the availability of test results: these results were available to officers of the authority, the School Psychological Service and the Remedial Service. The Education Committee saw only the overall marks, not the marks for individual schools. Heads and teachers saw only overall marks and their own marks, not those of other schools. Results were never made available in a routine way to parents, but three authorities would make individual pupils' scores available if asked. Nowhere were the results published in any form or made available to the media.

Testing procedures were most frequently carried out in the children's final year in the infant school. All the authorities who conducted county-wide testing administered reading tests at this age, and one did additional testing also. This is a year earlier than recommended by Bullock, who in 1974 stated: 'Our own view, therefore, is that if tests are used they should be introduced not earlier than the middle of the first term of the junior school and not later than the beginning of the second term.' The reason for testing rather earlier is closely connected with the reasoning behind the testing programme. At its earliest stage, testing is used principally for screening purposes to discover children with learning difficulties and particularly reading problems. After the screening children are further investigated, and some are identified for special help which may involve the allocation of resources to particular schools. It is administratively convenient to make this allocation at the beginning of the child's first year in the junior school.

The situation current in the authorities discussed in this study would appear to echo that found by Gipps and Wood (1981):

> Programmes which set out originally with screening as their purpose, as often than not have monitoring added, perhaps as a political response and then most recently with cuts to the fore, have had allocation of resources added as well.

All the authorities that tested at 6+ (top infants) tested primarily for screening purposes to discover children with reading difficulties. All of the authorities claimed that this screening was followed by further investigation of some children and extra help being offered to them. The secondary reason for this testing was monitoring of standards. Monitoring was followed by extra attention being paid to some schools and possibly extra resources being allocated. In all the authorities but one there were no rules about the connection between test scores and this allocation, and the apparent absence of guiding principles had become a very sensitive issue in some areas. In the remaining authority, the main purpose of testing was the allocation of resources in the form of hours of help given to schools by the Remedial Service. It is, however, a very unusual arrangement. Of the six authorities who tested at six, three also test at eleven. At this point, reasons for testing become more varied but the trend would appear to be in the direction of screening becoming less important and the monitoring of standards becoming more important. Even though selection at eleven is now unusual, the transition from primary to secondary education is still regarded as an important landmark and this may well be why some LEAs like the idea of a 'stocktaking' at this point. Also, even where there is no selection to particular schools based on testing at eleven, children may be allocated to different bands within the school on the strength of test results.

The most widely-used test for the screening of top infants is the Young Reading Test. Used for testing at this age, it is reasonably satisfactory. On a practical level it has the advantages of being cheap and quick and easy to administer. It also tests reading for meaning and it discriminates satisfactorily at the bottom end of the distribution, both of which are important features in tests used for screening.

The authorities who do not screen whole year groups use different methods to identify children who need additional help, but all operate remedial and other support services irrespective of whether they have screening procedures. One authority has adopted a procedure which is very similar to that which Bullock recommended when testing is primarily for the purpose of identifying poor readers. This recommendation involved the careful observation and recording of performance by the teacher, followed by testing procedures for some children. The scheme is run by the area educational psychologists, who advise teachers both with the initial identification of children who may have learning difficulties and with choice of appropriate tests. In the remaining authorities, without testing procedures, the support services offer extra provision for certain children and advice for teachers, usually at the request of the school. Here the burden of initial identification is placed firmly on the school, but with guidance from the specialist support services there is no reason to suppose that it is any less effective.

Reading tests in schools

It has already been established that it is the testing of reading that dominates the testing programmes of junior schools. The children in over 90 per cent of classrooms came in contact with some form of reading test. Table 7.2 illustrates the frequency with which reading tests are used.

The most widespread practice is for the whole class to be tested either once or twice a year. This happens in just over 66 per cent of junior classrooms, but the children in nearly 11 per cent of classrooms are tested four times or more during the school year. Using only one test was the most frequent procedure but a substantial number used two tests, and just over 10 per cent used three or more. Testing, then, is very much a regular and established school activity.

The range of tests used in schools can be seen in Table 7.3. Although a wide variety of tests are used it is the overwhelming popularity of the Schonell and Burt Word-Recognition Tests that

Table 7.2 The use of reading tests

		N	%
Frequency			
Number of times per year whole class is tested	None	40	9.3
	One	111	25.9
	Two	172	40.2
	Three	58	13.6
	More	47	10.9
Number of different tests used	None	36	8.4
	One	191	44.6
	Two	156	36.4
	More	45	10.5
Number of classrooms 428			

stands out. The Schonell WRT was used in 33.9 per cent of class-rooms, and in a further 31.3 per cent the Burt WRT was used. In no classroom were both these tests used. The third most popular test, but a long way behind, was the Daniels and Diack Test of Reading

Table 7.3 Reading tests

Rank order of tests used	% Classrooms	Type; Ind/Group
Schonell Word-Recognition	33.9	I
Burt Word-Recognition	31.3	I
Daniels & Diack R E Test 12	16.4	G
Young/SPAR	14.5	G
GAP	11.0	G
NFER Reading Tests	6.8	G
Holborn	5.8	I
Schonell Sentence Reading	4.4	I
Daniels & Diack Test 1	4.0	I
Neale	3.7	I
Edinburgh	2.8	G
Widespan	2.1	G
Southgate	1.6	G
Nelson Primary Reading Test	1.4	G
Carver	1.4	G
McNally	0.9	G
Salford	0.9	G
Spooncer	0.7	G
Other (including 'home made' tests)	4.7	
Number of classrooms = 428		

Experience, which was used in rather more than 16 per cent of classrooms. This was followed by the Young Reading Test or the SPAR test and then the GAP test. No other test was used in as many as 10 per cent of classrooms.

The Daniels and Diack, Young/SPAR and GAP tests are all group tests and, unlike the Burt and Schonell WRTs, they place their emphasis on reading for meaning. In general, the schools do use them with appropriate children but unfortunately the Daniels and Diack test, the most popular of this type, has not been properly standardised and so it is not clear how much importance can be given to children's scores. Very few of the tests used included any diagnostic element. However, some of the 4.7 per cent of teachers who used tests so unusual that they had to be categorised as 'other' include, in some instances, testing procedures that could help teachers pinpoint which aspects of reading a child has grasped and those with which he may need help. Nevertheless, even if it is assumed that all the 'other' tests were of this sort, only a small proportion of teachers used diagnostic tests.

The dominance of word-recognition tests is shown emphatically by the data presented in Table 7.4. Not only is such a test used in over 70 per cent of classrooms: equally striking is the evidence that in nearly 33 per cent of classrooms teachers use either the Schonell or Burt WRTs and no other kind of testing procedure.

The very limited nature of the word-recognition tests was highlighted in the Bullock Report (DES, 1974). Since that date this sort of test has decreased in popularity in LEA testing programmes and it has been largely replaced by newer tests involving reading for meaning (Gipps and Wood, 1981). Word-recognition tests do no more than test a child's skill at decoding and are based on a simplistic model of

Table 7.4 Use of the Schonell and Burt Word-Recognition Tests

	N	% of all classes	% of classes where tests are used
Burt WR	134	31.3	34.2
Schonell WR	145	33.9	37.0
Either	279*	65.2	71.2
Classes where only a WRT is used	129	30.1	32.9
Classes where some other test is used	217	61.2	66.8

* No one used both.

the nature of reading. A child's score on such a test gives the teacher a very limited amount of information about a child's reading skill. In particular, it gives no indication of the extent of a child's understanding of the written word.

The Schonell WRT was never intended to be used to measure all aspects of a child's reading skills. Schonell himself says: 'Studies of the tests used show that this type of test can be a reasonably accurate way of estimating the level reached by a pupil in the *mechanics of reading*' (original emphasis). The criticism of the word-recognition tests must be directed principally at the way they are used rather than at the tests themselves. Although word-recognition tests have particular disadvantages, the other kinds of tests commonly used also have serious limitations. They may give an overall assessment of at least some aspect of reading ability but are not at all diagnostic in orientation. They can tell us if children are performing poorly or at a low level of achievement but they cannot tell us anything specific about the educational needs of these children. It is possible to use such tests in order to identify children, who can then be tested in detail by more complex and diagnostic procedures. However, this is in fact rarely done. A further complication is that a test that can, for example, give a score for both the most and least able pupils in a class of seven-year-olds may not discriminate very well at the top or bottom of the range. Even where tests do offer such discrimination, the approximately normal distribution of scores in such tests is not very appropriate for defining a cut-off point for children who need extra help or who have particular difficulties. This absence of a cut-off point that would help rank the levels of difficulty encountered by poor readers is related to the question of diagnosis. At the tail end of the distribution any cut-off point is unsatisfactory, as the children immediately to either side of it are likely to have much more in common with each other than they do with most other children in the group in which they have been placed. A poor score on most types of standardised reading tests, and particularly word-recognition tests, gives the teacher very little information about a child's ability and gives no indication at all about his strengths and weaknesses and what, if any, action needs to be taken.

The Schonell and Burt Word-Recognition Tests have the advantage that the same test can be administered to each child in the junior school and the same test can be used for any individual child every year he is in the school. This makes it possible to monitor the child's performance through the school and to compare different years and different teachers' classes. There is nothing essentially wrong with this activity as long as its very real limitations are realised.

All forms of reading tests that are not diagnostic in nature separate the activities of teaching reading and testing reading. The separation of the two activities limits the usefulness of the testing. Pumphrey (1977) claims that, ideally, 'The testing of children's reading skills and attainment is not an end in itself but is one means of promoting better reading' and, if used to best advantage, 'the testing of reading ceases to be an isolated aspect of the teacher's work. It is seen as an inevitable and indispensable aspect of competent instruction. The teaching and testing of reading can be considered as integral parts in a hypothesis testing situation.' In the great majority of schools, testing was not viewed in this way.

The problematic limitations of many reading tests, especially word-recognition tests, have been demonstrated in the serious criticisms levelled at them, but often schools create problems that are not inherent in the tests themselves. These tests and many others give a score in the form of a reading age. Reading ages always need to be considered in close conjunction with the chronological age of the child; otherwise they have very little meaning. A list of the reading ages of the children in 3C gives us no more than the crudest idea about either the general level of the class or individual children. The chronological age of the children in 3C may vary by up to twelve months and possibly more. If two individual children of the same reading age are taken for illustration, the consequences of not considering the reading age and chronological age together can be seen. Both may have a reading age of 7 years 10 months, but one child may be 9 years old and a little more than a year behind, while another child may be nearly 10 years old and be more than two years behind. A gap of this sort is regarded by most schools as giving cause for concern but it can be very easily overlooked. In many of the classrooms studied it was found that reading ages and chronological ages were not recorded together. In response to this criticism teachers may claim that the most important piece of information to be obtained from a reading test score from their point of view is whether or not a child is so significantly different from the rest of the class as to make it difficult for him to cope. There is some justification for regarding test scores in this way in classrooms where class teaching is the predominant teaching style. In most classrooms, however, children spend a very considerable amount of time working individually, not as members either of the class or of a group.

Many observational studies of classrooms, including the research reported here (Chapter 9) and the ORACLE study, *Inside the Primary Classroom* (Galton, Simon and Croll, 1980), have highlighted the extent to which children spend the school day working on their own. Where work is individualised, a child's test score is of greater assistance in planning suitable work if taken in conjunction with his age than if it is taken in conjunction with the general level of his class. The significance of a child's reading age and his teacher's assessment of his reading ability and the connection between the child's age relative to the class and his reading skills as perceived by his teacher have been considered in detail in Chapter 6.

Testing and children with learning difficulties

Re-examination of Table 7.1 shows that in 137 classrooms (among them a small number where only children with learning difficulties did tests) children with learning difficulties were tested more frequently than the rest of the class. The typical procedure was to use the same test on all children but to administer it more frequently to those with learning difficulties. Teachers probably feel that it is particularly important to get an objective measure of the progress made by children with learning difficulties. However, this is frequently done by using tests that are not diagnostic in orientation, so that teaching and testing are quite separate activities, not part of the same process. This would indicate that many teachers have a very generalised view of the skill of reading and its teaching. Testing is not used to identify particular areas of weakness which are then helped by a programme of remediation, the effectiveness of which is again tested. The process is more usually the giving of one, non-diagnostic test, often a word-recognition test, followed by 'practice' of the reading skills the child has not mastered, followed by more testing.

Well over half (57.3 per cent) of the children whom their teachers regarded as having special needs received additional help through withdrawal from the classroom. Most of this special help was with reading. The procedure for selecting children to receive special help usually consisted of a consideration of both test results and the opinion of the class teacher. In a few instances where no testing was done, the decision was based on teacher recommendation alone. In only one case were test results the sole basis for selection. The procedure in all the remaining schools took both factors into account: both school test results and results of tests administered as part of an LEA screening procedure were considered.

During the research twenty-five remedial teachers who were withdrawing children from the regular class for extra help with reading were interviewed and asked about testing procedures they used. Fourteen used no testing procedures in addition to those conducted in the regular class. In one instance this was because a Neale analysis was done on all the children and this was regarded as sufficient. Ten teachers employed tests that were, at least in part, diagnostic, usually calling in expert advice from either the remedial or the advisory service. There was a marked difference between testing procedures used with the help of experts and those used by remedial teachers alone. In view of the desirability for testing and teaching to be part of the same process it is very likely that variations in skill in testing are accompanied by similar variations in skill in teaching.

Although non-diagnostic tests give only a limited amount of information, if the purpose of the test is for initial screening or monitoring of standards they may be perfectly suitable. As part of a programme of identification and remediation of reading difficulties, however, they leave a lot to be desired.

Teachers' views on testing: reaction to test scores

Having established that the use of standardised tests is a very widespread practice we must now consider the part they play in the life of the classroom. Of particular interest is the influence that test results have on the class teacher's assessments of children's achievements and abilities. There is a substantial body of research into discrepancies between teachers' opinions of a child's capabilities and his score on standardised tests, and opinion on this issue has tended to fall into two directly opposite camps: those who believe in test scores and those who put their trust in teachers' opinions. To take either of these stances would be to take a simplistic view both of a child's ability and performance and of the nature of standardised testing procedures. There is no need to regard either the teacher or the tests as definitely right or wrong. Both teacher opinion and test score can be viewed as pieces of information about the child in the classroom. The real capabilities of a child are not going to be adequately described either by one test score or by the isolated opinion of one teacher. Both test scores and teacher observations can together be used to gain more insight into the capabilities and achievements of children. A test score cannot fully describe all a child's abilities but used as one piece of information among many others available to the teacher, it may provide extra insight into the functioning of the child. This is particularly true when a child's score is higher than the teacher expected. In this instance a good performance by a child can encourage the teacher to discover abilities in that child which had not previously been recognised. It is more fruitful to ask, 'What part do tests play in the life of the junior classroom?' than, 'Who is right, teacher or test?'

In this study the issue of discrepancies between teachers' assessments of children and their scores on standardised tests is investigated from the point of view of the teachers: just as teachers' perceptions of special needs are a focus of concern, so teachers' own reactions to mismatch are of particular interest. One of the main objectives was to discover the frequency with which teachers experience mismatch, the types of tests associated with these discrepancies and the teachers' reactions to children achieving unexpected scores. The connection between test scores, teachers' assessments and other pupil characteristics is dealt with in other chapters.

Table 7.5 Discrepancies reported by teachers between teacher opinion and test score

Frequency of discrepancy	Reading tests	Reasoning tests	Achievement tests
Usually	5.4	0.9	0.6
Sometimes	31.8	18.7	5.2
Infrequently	25.8	12.2	3.8
Total mentioning mismatch	63.0	31.8	9.6
Teachers using test	392 (100%)	115 (100%)	289 (100%)

The data presented in Table 7.5 gives a clear indication of the frequency with which teachers experience discrepancies between their expectations and children's actual test scores. First, it must be remembered how these responses were elicited. They were replies to the questions:

'Do you find that test results ever conflict with your own opinion?'
'Which sorts of test?'
'How often?'

By asking this type of question we hoped to discover what teachers actually thought about the issue rather than how they would react to a predetermined set of alternative responses, many of which, especially those that lie outside the frame of reference that teachers use when considering the question of testing, they may never previously have thought about. The frequency with which discrepancies were reported is illustrated in Table 7.5.

Reading tests were used in over 90 per cent of the classrooms in the sample, and just over 63 per cent of the teachers involved (over twice as many who mention mismatch with any other type of test) claimed that they experienced mismatch on some occasions. At first sight this may seem to indicate a degree of dissatisfaction with testing procedures, but viewed from a slightly different angle the picture is quite different. Any test is subject to a certain degree of test error, and so occasionally a child will get a 'wrong' score. With this in mind, if the teachers who experienced mismatch only infrequently are added to those who reported no mismatch at all this means that 62.5 per cent of teachers using reading tests find that children only rarely have surprising scores. Only just over 5 per cent of teachers said that children's test scores usually surprised them. Overall, this would seem to indicate quite a high level of agreement between teacher opinion and reading test results.

Achievement test results produced the lowest incidence of mismatch. It is this type of test which is, generally speaking, closest to the day-to-day activities of the classroom and which best tests the knowledge and skills which form a substantial part of the curriculum. A mathematics test, for example, can test precisely the skills that the teacher has taught and the child has been using in classroom work. The relationship between the material and skills taught and the content of the test is at its closest in achievement tests, and so teachers are not often surprised by their pupils' results. Although reading is of central importance and concern in the junior classroom it is not actually taught in most classrooms to most children. It is rather an essential tool that is being improved through practice and through being used to pursue other classroom learning. Teachers are mostly looking at the results that children achieve by the use they make of reading rather than at the reading skill itself. It is understandable that reading-test scores can and do surprise teachers, since some children use their skills to good advantage in the classroom and others do not.

Perhaps unexpectedly, only 32 per cent of teachers using reasoning tests mentioned mismatch. The most likely explanation for the fact that this figure is appreciably lower than the mismatch figure drawn from reading tests lies in the frequency and centrality of the testing of reading in the junior classroom and the firmness of impression and expectation that the teacher is thus led to develop in this area of the children's skills. Reasoning tests, by contrast, are a regular feature in far fewer junior classrooms: their most frequent occurrence comes later, at the end of the fourth-year, and then at the request of the LEA or secondary school. It is perhaps unfamiliarity with them that makes some teachers uncertain exactly what skills are measured by reasoning tests.

The testing of reading, however, although it may form part of LEA testing programmes, is also usually part of the school's own policy and a regular feature of classroom life, much more to the forefront of teachers' minds when they are considering the issue of testing and test scores.

Teachers' reactions to mismatch

How do teachers who experience discrepancies between their estimation of a child's capability and his test score react to this discrepancy? It would appear that it is possible to divide teachers' reactions into two basic types – the reactions that offer *explanations* of the mismatch and the responses that are expressed in terms of the *actions* that the teachers would take when pupils achieve surprising scores.

Over 36 per cent of teachers offered explanations in terms of dissatisfaction with the tests, saying that tests are generally unsatisfactory or wrong and are less accurate than teacher perceptions, or they described tests as being unreliable or having other technical weaknesses (Table 7.6). Teachers giving these explanations prefer their own judgments to test scores. However, some teachers (26.2 per

Table 7.6 Reactions to discrepancies between teacher opinion and standardised test scores

Explanations and actions	% of teachers using standardised tests
Tests are generally unsatisfactory/wrong/less accurate than teacher perceptions	17.6
Tests are unreliable, other technical weaknesses	18.9
Children have good/bad days, can be nervous/lucky	31.5
Cheating	6.8
Tests are likely to be more accurate than teacher judgments	21.7
Children's behaviour/attitude may mislead teacher	7.2
Age factor in test standardisation	0.7
Ignore test result	5.4
Retest	11.0
Observe carefully/reappraisal	20.3
Try harder/easier work	12.1
Number of teachers using tests = 402	

cent) do tend to favour test results in preference to their own opinion, saying that children's behaviour and attitude or age may mislead the teacher and that, on the whole, tests are likely to be more accurate than teacher judgment. A third group (33.9 per cent) do not come down firmly in favour of either the teacher or the test as 'right' but seek explanations of discrepancy in terms of factors that hinder a child from achieving his 'correct' score. Explanations of this sort include assertions that cheating takes place, that performance is affected by nerves and that children have 'good' or 'bad' days and can be 'lucky' or 'unlucky'. Here the teacher neither rejects the test score as the more accurate indicator of ability nor modifies her opinion of the child but explains the child's test score by regarding it as an unusual performance. These teachers do not firmly reject the test score out of hand but they stay with their original opinion of a child; so it would be fair to interpret this position as indicating a tendency to disbelieve the test score. When the teachers who firmly reject the test result are added to those who tend to disbelieve, this accounts for approximately 70 per cent of those teachers who experience mismatch.

When, however, we look at reactions in terms of actions that teachers say they take in response to discrepancies we find a slightly different picture, with the teachers who responded to the question in terms of actions showing reluctance to reject the test score completely. Only 5.4 per cent of teachers said that they would ignore the test result. Nearly 11 per cent said that they would retest, thus expressing a measure of disbelief in the test score, but 20.3 per cent said that they would observe the child carefully with a view to reappraisal and 12.1 per cent said they would change the type of work the child was doing and try either harder or easier work. This would appear to be an indication that the teacher is prepared not necessarily to accept the test score as 'right', but nevertheless to regard it as a piece of information about a child that deserves to be taken seriously and which may lead the teacher to reassess her opinions of a child.

The discussion so far has been concerned with teachers' overall reactions to any sort of discrepancy between their own assessments and test scores. In his study of elementary school teachers in the USA, Salmon-Cox (1981) claimed that teachers reacted very differently towards test scores that were unexpectedly high and those that were unexpectedly low. Although on the whole these teachers preferred their own opinions of children's ability to standardised test scores and considered a poor result on a test to be insufficient evidence for regarding a child to be less able than they had thought, they were on the other hand, frequently prepared to regard a higher than expected score as an indication of hidden talent. In the present study teachers' reactions to test scores were elicited by open-ended questions asked in an interview rather than by multiple-choice questions on a questionnaire. The majority of teachers in the present research (61.2 per cent) reported no differentiation in their reactions to various types of discrepancy. However, in the minority of cases where teachers did differentiate, their reactions were similar to those reported by Salmon-Cox. These teachers were more likely to favour the test result rather than their previous opinions when the test scores were higher than expected and to regard the tests themselves as unsatisfactory when the scores were not as good as expected.

On balance, teachers appeared relatively content with the tests used in their classrooms despite the shortcomings of some of the most popular. Only a minority of teachers wanted to see more or different tests and only 4 per cent were against testing in principle. Teachers' reactions to test scores would seem to indicate that, while taking scores seriously, they regard them as only one indication of ability, to be placed alongside others.

8 Provision

Central to both the Warnock Report and the 1981 Education Act is the idea that children with special educational needs are children who require some form of special provision. The Report and the Act both, therefore, make explicit the policy of describing children in terms of their needs rather than classifying them according to their disabilities. As a result special provision can more readily be defined in relation to the special needs of children. Details of the nature of the special provision children are receiving will be discussed later in the chapter when the various types of provision for particular sorts of difficulties are considered. For the moment the central concern is the extent to which pupils described by their teachers as having special needs do, in fact, receive special provision. It is hoped that this survey may give a new perspective to the question of both definition and incidence of special needs.

In Table 8.1 figures are presented for: (a) the numbers of children currently receiving special help, (b) the numbers of children for whom teachers would like special help or additional special help,

Table 8.1 Provision for pupils with special needs

	N	% of nominated pupils	% of total sample
Pupils receiving extra help beyond ordinary class provision	1303	56.2	10.6
All pupils for whom teachers would like (more) extra help	1204	44.2	8.3
Pupils not currently receiving extra help for whom teachers would like such help	504	21.8	4.1
Pupils either receiving extra help or for whom teachers would like extra help	1807	78.0	14.7

(c) the numbers of children for whom teachers would like special help but are not currently receiving any such help (these children also appear in group (b)), and, (d) the total of pupils either receiving special help or for whom their teachers would like help (this is the total of categories (a) and (c)).

For the purposes of Table 8.1 special provision is defined as anything beyond the ordinary teaching activities of the classroom. It includes extra help given by the teacher at lunchtime or break, remedial reading taught in a separate class and attendance outside the school at, for example, a child guidance clinic or reading centre. Also included are a small number of instances where the ordinary classroom activities of the child have been devised according to specialist advice such as that from an educational psychologist or remedial reading specialist. Thus defined, special provision varies from something which is a very small part of a child's school day and of which, in some instances, he may not be aware, to very extensive special provision such as the help of a full-time auxiliary or daily attendance at a reading centre. Over half of the pupils nominated by their teachers as having special needs do receive some sort of special help, 56.2 per cent of the nominated pupils, or 10.6 per cent of the total of pupils in the classes studied. In the cases of 44.2 per cent of the pupils we discussed with teachers, the teacher felt that the child needed special help or needed more special help than he was receiving. Thus, 8.3 per cent of pupils in the classes studied had special needs which their teachers felt were not being completely met. About half of these pupils were children who were not receiving any form of special provision, so that 21.8 per cent of the pupils with special needs and 4.1 per cent of all pupils were considered by their teachers to need extra help but were not receiving such help. It can be calculated from the figures in Table 8.1 that of pupils currently receiving special help 40 per cent were considered by their teachers to need more help than they were receiving and that among pupils getting no special help 59.7 per cent were thought by their teachers to need help.

The figures presented in Table 8.1 highlight a possible different perspective on the incidence of pupils with special educational needs from that presented earlier. If special needs are needs for special provision, then adding together the number of pupils currently getting special provision and the number of children not receiving such help but regarded by their teachers as needing it gives an estimate of 14.7 per cent of the total sample of pupils as having need for special provision. This means that just over one in five of the pupils described as having special needs were neither receiving special help nor regarded by their teachers as needing such help. These pupils will be investigated further and the nature of their possible special needs discussed later in the chapter.

The majority of children receiving special educational provision are getting help from the school's own resources, typically being withdrawn from the regular class for special help with reading. Similarly, in most of the instances where teachers say a child needs more special provision they are referring to this sort of 'in-school' provision. However, a number of pupils are getting help from outside their schools. This sort of help includes visiting a child guidance clinic or reading centre and seeing a visiting remedial specialist or speech therapist at the school, and it has also been defined here to include instances of a child's own teacher following a work programme or similar scheme with advice from an outside specialist such as an educational psychologist.

In Table 8.2 the incidence of this sort of special help is shown, together with the numbers of cases where a teacher would like such help, or more of such help, for a child. As the table shows, 17.7 per cent of pupils with special needs, making up 3.3 per cent of the total sample, receive some sort of special provision from outside the school. In the case of 9.2 per cent of pupils with special needs or 1.7 per cent of the total sample, teachers say they would like, or would like more, help provided by agencies external to the school.

In total, there were 589 pupils who either were getting such provision or in their teachers' eyes would be helped by it. These

Table 8.2 Provision requiring 'out of school' resources

	N	% of nominated pupils	% of total sample
Pupils receiving help involving 'out of school' resources	411	17.7	3.3
All pupils for whom teachers would like (more) 'out of school' resources	214	9.2	1.7
Pupils not currently receiving 'out of school' help for whom teachers would like such help	178	7.7	1.4
Pupils either receiving 'out of school' help or for whom their teachers would like such help	589	25.4	4.8

children constitute a quarter of the pupils regarded by their teachers as having special needs and about one in twenty of the total sample. Considered from another angle, this means that with nearly three-quarters of the children they consider to have special educational needs teachers do not want help from outside the school. There is a strong suggestion here that teachers believe that, for the most part, meeting special needs is the responsibility of the school and school staff. The willingness of teachers to attempt to cope with special needs in their own classrooms is further emphasised by their expressed desire to keep in their classrooms a large majority of children for whom special school could be a realistic alternative. Teachers thought that under 5 per cent of their pupils with special needs would be better off in a special school; that is, they were of the opinion that a special school would be a more appropriate placement than a regular class for fewer than one child in a hundred now in the junior school. These issues have already been dealt with more fully in Chapter 5.

Special needs and the LEAs

Teachers do indeed have to both assess and meet the special educational needs of many of their pupils unaided. There are, however, a large number of support services in all areas upon which schools can call. Most of these are provided by the local education authority but others are offered by the district health authority or the social services departments and others by the LEA in partnership with the DHA and/or social services. Despite the fact that all LEAs operate within the same statutory framework there is very considerable variation with regard to educational provision. The ten local authorities in the study vary considerably in the sorts of provision made available for children with special educational needs and they also vary in policies for identification and remediation and the extent to which pupils are placed in separate provision outside the normal school. Some services are provided by all authorities (though some much more lavishly than others) while others are specific to the authority, determined by different local circumstances, perceived needs and levels of funding. All LEAs in the study provide a school psychological service, an advisory service and a remedial service. Some provide services such as an ethnic minority support service but others not. However, even the universally provided services can vary significantly in the functions they fulfil and in the type of service that they offer to schools. This traditional variation in policy and provision between authorities means that there have been many responses to the Warnock Report and that local authorities vary in the ways in which they are implementing the 1981 Education Act. It is also clear that the previously existing baseline of types of provision will continue to exert a considerable influence on the way an authority deals with special educational needs.

The impact of Warnock

The Warnock Report had been greeted enthusiastically by all the LEA officers to whom we spoke and we were told that it had been widely welcomed in the authorities. Previously, special education had not been in the educational limelight, and the Report created more interest in special education both publicly and, more particularly, in the education committees. The following quotation is very typical of what we were told:

> 'Policy in relation to special education did not change dramatically but Warnock gave a definite boost to things that were already happening and focused more attention on special education and more interest generally is taken in this area of education, especially by the education committee.' (AEO with responsibility for Special Education)

The above quotation is typical both in its claim that the Warnock Report has revitalised the area of special education and also in the suggestion that it has not produced, nor is it likely to produce, any very dramatic changes. In general, the LEA officers believed that there would not be any major changes within the authority, since their own particular LEA policy had been determined by the same climate of opinion which also resulted in the Warnock Report. By the late 1970s, most of the authorities were already in the process of instigating integration programmes, particularly in the form of moving children from special schools into units attached to ordinary schools.

Services for the hearing-impaired

It is in the field of hearing impairment that perhaps most progress has been made towards integration of 'handicapped' children into regular schools. All the LEAs operate a service for the hearing-impaired, although the structure and the organisation vary. One authority has a most unusual arrangement in which the 'special educational needs service' is an amalgamation of two support services – the remedial reading service and services for hearing-impaired children. The other authorities all operate services that are exclusive to the hearing-impaired, usually in collaboration with the district health authority. Partially-hearing children were among the first of the handicapped to be integrated in any numbers into ordinary schools. This provision pre-dates Warnock and has subsequently, in many instances, acted as a model for the establishment of various sorts of unit provision. There has been an overall increase, over the last ten years, in the number of units for the hearing-impaired attached to ordinary schools in the ten LEAs, although in fact there has been a recent decline in some areas both in the number of units and in the number of children in them. This decline has three chief causes, all facilitating the increasing integration of children with hearing difficulties into regular class-rooms. First, medical advances have resulted in the early diagnosis and surgical cure of some children so that they do not experience hearing difficulties at school. Second, the improvements in electronic hearing aids and changes in ideas about effective teaching techniques have made the integration of hearing-impaired children much easier.

Within the LEAs the services for the hearing-impaired undertake the staffing of units attached to primary schools, advise teachers who have hearing-impaired children in their classroom and monitor the children's progress. The support they offer to the ordinary school is expanding as an increasing number of children with hearing impairments are placed in ordinary classrooms. In addition, as the number of children in the units declines, the service tends to spread its net in a variety of directions to include provision at nursery and at further education levels, and to offer services to children with language and communication disorders.

Services for the visually-impaired

Services for the visually-impaired are an area of expansion in several authorities. Half of the authorities visited have either newly-created schemes or recently-expanded provision. There would seem to be two main reasons for this. First, there was the realisation that visually-impaired children can be educated in units attached to ordinary schools or even integrated into the regular classroom, and second, authorities are now anxious to save money by reducing the number of children educated outside the authority, and providing for their visually-impaired children in regular schools, though expensive, is considerably cheaper than placing them in privately-run establishments. Here is an unusual example of educational principle and financial expediency both demanding the same course of action.

Provision for children with physical disabilities and health problems

None of the ten authorities offers an organised service to schools to help them cope with physically handicapped children or children with health problems. If the education authority does offer help it is in the form of welfare assistants, not specialists. Support may be provided by the health authority, but not the education authority. It is the health authorities too who are also largely responsible for identifying the children who are offered help by the services for the visually-impaired and hearing-impaired. In this area there is much less emphasis on a school having to identify children and ask for help. Most, though not all, of the children are identified before school age and begin their school life with special help.

Provision for children with severe behaviour problems

In most of the ten authorities there has been a substantial growth in provision for the maladjusted, which is still continuing. One authority opened a new special school in 1982. Here, the education committee and the officers were both reluctant to take this action but, in the end, relented under pressure from the schools. It is significant that the expansion of provision for the maladjusted is taking the form of increased places in special schools and the establishment of units which are not attached to schools, whereas children with other handicaps – especially physical handicaps and sensory impairments – are increasingly being integrated into regular schools. This development, which is consistent with the attitudes among teachers to the inclusion of maladjusted pupils in their classes reported in Chapter 5, suggests that the schools themselves can exert a powerful influence on LEA policy even when the schools are moving against the consensus of informed opinion.

Another developing type of provision is that offered by units for disruptive pupils. These units cater for pupils whose behaviour cannot be contained in ordinary classrooms. Such children are not necessarily maladjusted and nor are they likely to be the subject of statements. These changes acknowledge that the special provision must take the form of changing the environment as well as attempting to change the child.

Special needs in ordinary schools

Despite the enthusiasm for the Warnock Report it was very noticeable that the Report's suggestion that special needs should be seen as a continuum which might include up to 20 per cent of the school population rather than the under 2 per cent currently in special provision, and would therefore be largely dealt with by ordinary schools, has made little impact within the authorities. Thinking about special education is still dominated by a consideration of the children who have traditionally been the concern of this section of the school system, and the role of ordinary schools is mainly seen in terms of what they can offer these children rather than in terms of any new initiatives for the benefit of pupils who would always be in the regular school. It is clear, for example, that the claim that there are adequate resources for special educational needs refers to children who fall into the traditional categories of handicap. In all ten of the authorities, officers could point to programmes or new appointments which were directed at the 2 per cent of the population traditionally the concern of special education, but only two of the authorities had any new initiatives for helping the 20 per cent considered by Warnock to have special educational needs in the ordinary classroom.

In determining the staffing levels in their schools, LEAs take the circumstances of particular schools into account. Schools in educational priority areas, schools with a high proportion of children for whom English is a second language, and schools who have 'handicapped' children or who have undesirable buildings may all get additional staff allocations over and above the standard level of LEA

99

provision. Only very unusually are heads directed about the use to be made of the staff in their schools. Heads organise their staff in the light of their professional judgment. A common course of action is to use at least a proportion of any teacher time available (after the staffing of classes has been secured) to operate some sort of remedial provision through withdrawal. Allocation of teacher time to remedial work is, therefore, a decision more usually made at school than at local authority level. This being the case, any decision made at County Hall in relation to staffing levels cannot be seen as being directed at reducing remedial provision in the schools, yet it may indeed have this effect.

Just under 56 per cent (55.8 per cent) of the heads interviewed claimed that cutbacks in LEA spending in 1981 had affected the way in which they dealt with special needs, and nearly 41 per cent (40.9 per cent) said that cutbacks had had a greater impact on the provision for children with special educational needs than on other school activities. Because there are typically no special remedial posts, remedial work in schools is frequently done by part-time teachers or may be done by a deputy head teacher with only part of a teaching timetable.

If any reduction occurs in the number of part-time teaching hours available or if a deputy has a full teaching load this can mean that there is no-one available to offer extra assistance to children with special needs. The provision that schools are able to make for children needing remedial help has not been cut back by direct LEA policy; nevertheless, many head teachers feel that it is because of cutbacks in educational expenditure that they cannot offer the provision they would like. Only 18 per cent of heads did not want to make different or additional provision. All the rest would have liked to be able to offer more, especially in the form of extra help with remedial reading. Nearly 40 per cent of heads would have liked to offer more of this type of help through withdrawal from the regular class, and over a quarter would have liked help to be given in the classroom setting. There was a decided lack of optimism about the possibility of being able to bring about the desired changes, with only 4 per cent confident of success and a further 16 per cent showing some optimism, but 76 per cent feeling that they would not be able to offer the standard range of services that they considered to be necessary.

The remedial reading service

In spite of the heads' regrets over the level of remedial provision they are able to offer, all ten LEAs do provide services to assist teachers in coping with children with special needs. The organisation and detailed functions of remedial services can vary appreciably, but the main concentration is on offering help to children with reading problems and their teachers.

In one particular authority, junior schools are allocated a certain number of hours from the remedial service on the basis, principally, of reading test results. The support offered takes the form of a remedial teacher who withdraws children from the regular class, mainly for extra reading. This system works in much the same way as having a remedial teacher in the school but the remedial services teacher is employed by, and is responsible to, the service rather than the head teacher and cannot be directed by the head to other duties. This particular system is unusual in that it is organised from County Hall to work in the schools, not at the request of the head teacher but as a matter of course. More typically, remedial and advisory services wait for the head teacher to invite them into the school, a manner of proceeding that emphasises how important teachers are in the initial assessment of children.

Several authorities reported recent changes in the organisation and functioning of advisory and remedial services. Until recently the remedial services had provided peripatetic teachers to help individual children through withdrawal but had now ceased to do this and instead had expanded their advisory role in the hope of enabling class teachers to cope more efficiently with all the children in their classes, so that eventually they would not need to have particular children withdrawn for help from visiting specialists. Where the remedial service still does have a teaching role it now tends to concentrate its limited resources on particular types of difficulty, especially on children who are diagnosed as having specific reading difficulties rather than more general problems of slow learning. Remedial services that operate in this way argue that by concentrating their attention on this type of child they can make very positive improvements in a child's performance in a relatively short time and so do the maximum amount of good in the limited time available. This does, of course, have the effect of placing the reading and other difficulties of the all-round slow learners very firmly in the hands of the class teacher.

Other non-teaching functions of the remedial service can include offering advice and materials in relation to the testing of reading and reading schemes and the provision of in-service courses. This change in function to a more general advisory role is illustrated by the fact that, of the 1898 children in the sample who were thought by their teachers to have learning difficulties, the remedial services were directly consulted about only 163 (8.6 per cent) individual children, though their advice may well have helped teachers to cope with many more.

With the aim of increasing teacher competence in coping with children with learning difficulties, one metropolitan authority that has severely restricted the teaching commitment of its remedial and advisory services has introduced in-service courses for teachers, run by these services in collaboration with the school psychological service. It is intended that all primary schools should have at least one senior member of staff who has attended a course and who will become responsible for training the other teachers at the school. The first year of this training scheme was monitored and assessed as part of the current research project (Brooks, 1983). The course proved to be popular with the first batch of teachers who attended and was regarded by them as being very useful.

The school psychological service

All LEAs in the study also operate a school psychological service, and all at least share in the responsibility for providing a child or family guidance service, but the level of provision varies appreciably. Several authorities have appointed additional psychologists since 1978 in response, first, to the Warnock Report's recommendation that provision in this area be improved and, second, to the increased workload (especially in the preparation of statements) that implementation of the Act has brought with it. Inevitably, the support that the school psychological service can offer to schools must in part be determined by staffing levels. Where there is only a small number of psychologists, the service can operate only on a crisis intervention basis, assessing children and recommending placement. Where the service is well staffed it is possible for the SPS to advise and support teachers in coping with a variety of children's problems. The service has always played a key role in the provision for children with special needs. The implementation of the Act is making its work even more crucial involving as this does the preparation of statements, regular reviews of children in special schools and the retention in ordinary classrooms of an increasing number of children who would previously have been placed in special schools. To some extent, the direction the service's work will take will be determined by the new legislation; but the levels of staffing determined by LEA policy and differing widely from area to area will also have a powerful influence on how particular services will operate.

The school psychological service is concerned with children who have every sort of special need, but it is particularly important in relation to children with learning difficulties and behaviour problems. These are the most numerous of the special needs and the ones that teachers least wish to be confronted with.

It might have been supposed that teachers would consult the SPS most frequently about children with multiple difficulties, but this does not appear to be the case. The most likely explanation for this is that teachers are more reluctant to have maladjusted children in their classes than pupils with any other type of handicap. They are therefore more likely to consult an EP about such a child both because they require advice on coping with the child and also because such contact may be the first step towards removing the child from the classroom.

As is the case with most of a junior school's external business, it is the head who negotiates with the SPS and it is extremely unusual for a class teacher to be able to make individual contact with an EP. Although it is the head who actually contacts the SPS and asks an EP to visit the school to look at a child or discuss his difficulties, it is typically the class teacher who will set this process in motion, when, having recognised that a child is experiencing difficulties, she consults the head. The role of the class teacher, then, is extremely important, as a child cannot receive help from the SPS unless the school contacts the service.

There is undoubtedly a desire on the part of both heads and class teachers to see more of their EP. In most authorities, nearly all contact between schools and SPS is about individual children who have been referred. Many teachers would appreciate more contact of a more informal nature for advice on individual children and also more generally on how to cope with children with special needs. Over half the class teachers (54.7 per cent) would have liked to receive more direct help from their EP in connection with particular children, and

60.5 per cent would have liked more help of a general nature from the SPS. Both heads and teachers felt that they did not receive as much help from the SPS as they would have liked because the EP was too busy and they suffered from a general lack of opportunity to extend contacts. Very few felt that the SPS were unwilling or unco-operative, but in many areas there were insufficient EPs to offer schools the type of service they would like.

Provision made by the school

Despite the help offered by the LEAs and their support services it is clear that, for the most part, special needs are met, or an attempt is made to meet them, within the school. In fact, it is not at all uncommon for a teacher to have a child with special needs in her classroom and to receive no help of any kind in dealing with the child and not even to consult other members of staff about him. Over 30 per cent of their pupils with special needs had not been discussed consultatively by their class teachers. This very much highlights the isolation of the classroom, which has been a major theme of other recent research into the activities of the primary classroom, particularly the ORACLE programme (Galton, Simon and Croll, 1980). Teachers do consult with other class teachers, with the head and with the remedial teacher if the school has one, but to a limited extent. Even in schools that have a remedial teacher, only 40 per cent of children with special needs were discussed with her. This may well be linked to the nature of the provision made for these children, which usually involves withdrawing the child from the class. Although isolation is very much a characteristic of the junior classroom, there is no reason to suppose that teachers like this situation. Teachers enjoyed being interviewed during the research and especially liked the opportunity to talk about their pupils.

Children with learning difficulties

Most children with special educational needs in the ordinary school have learning difficulties of some kind: these problems are usually dominated by poor reading skills. By far the most common form of special educational provision available in the junior schools in our

Table 8.3 Withdrawal for help with learning difficulties

	N	% of all learning difficulties	% of total sample
Pupils withdrawn from the regular class for help with learning difficulties	1087	57.3	8.8
Pupils with learning difficulties not withdrawn	811	42.7	6.6
All pupils with learning difficulties	1898	100	15.4

study was withdrawal from the regular class for special help with learning problems: 56 per cent of the schools had withdrawal of this kind on a regular basis and a further 8 per cent had a limited amount of such withdrawal. Table 8.3 shows the proportion of pupils with learning difficulties who are withdrawn for special help. Of the 1898 pupils described by their teachers as having learning difficulties, over 57 per cent were withdrawn from the regular class at some point in the school week: this means that nearly 9 per cent of the pupils in the classes studied were withdrawn for help with learning problems. However, 42.7 per cent of pupils described by their teachers as having learning difficulties were not withdrawn. These figures refer only to pupils who were withdrawn for help with their academic work.

Some of the pupils who are described in the table as not being withdrawn may leave their classes at some time for help with behavioural or emotional problems or for help with physical and sensory difficulties. Help from specialists such as speech therapists and peripatetic teachers of the blind and deaf has been excluded from the category of academic help. The content of the special help received by these pupils is set out in Table 8.4. As before, reading and related

Table 8.4 The content of special help received by children

	N	% of pupils withdrawn
Children getting special help with:		
Reading, writing or spelling	1062	97.7
Mathematics or number work	140	12.9
Other areas of the curriculum	32	2.9
Total pupils withdrawn:	1087	

activities dominate the teachers' and schools' definitions of learning difficulties in the junior school. Virtually all the pupils withdrawn for special help with their learning problems are getting help relating to reading, writing and spelling. Nearly 13 per cent receive help with mathematics or number work, and just under 3 per cent help with other areas of the curriculum. These categories, of course, overlap: most of the pupils receiving help with mathematics or other areas of the curriculum are also receiving help with reading, writing or spelling.

The amount of time spent out of the regular class by children withdrawn for special help with learning difficulties is relevant not only to the amount of special help they receive but also to questions about the nature of such special help and the part it plays in the education offered in the ordinary classroom. In general, children are withdrawn from the regular class for a relatively small part of their school week. Table 8.5 shows that for almost a quarter of pupils withdrawn for special help with learning difficulties this withdrawal amounts to an hour or less out of their school week.

For over a third of the pupils this withdrawal is for between one and two hours a week, and for another fifth between two and three hours. In other words, four-fifths of the children withdrawn from the regular class to receive help with learning difficulties spend rarely more than three hours a week and usually a good deal less in their withdrawal group. Table 8.5 gives no indication of how this time is divided up during the week, but short periods of half-an-hour or less spaced evenly throughout the week are by far the most common. In addition

Table 8.5 Length of time spent out of the regular class

Amount of time per week spent withdrawn from the regular class by children with learning difficulties	No. of pupils	% of pupils withdrawn
30 minutes or less	42	3.9
30 minutes–1 hour	218	20.1
1 hour–2 hours	396	36.4
2 hours–3 hours	222	20.4
3 hours–5 hours	163	15.0
5 hours–10 hours	27	2.5
10 hours +	19	1.7
Total pupils withdrawn:	1087	100

to these pupils, a further 15 per cent receive between three and five hours' special help in the week, making a total of over 95 per cent of pupils withdrawn for this sort of special help who are withdrawn for not more than an hour a day or its equivalent. A small number of pupils are withdrawn for between five and ten hours a week and a smaller number still for more than ten hours from an average school week.

This discussion has so far avoided the term 'remedial' to describe this sort of special help with learning difficulties although, in the schools we studied, this term was almost universally used to describe withdrawal from the ordinary class for special help with academic work. There is considerable discussion over the kinds of special provision within ordinary schools which can appropriately be called remedial. In its most general use the term is sometimes applied to any kind of special help offered to children who are substantially behind in academic subjects, whatever the nature of their difficulty or the type of special help they are receiving. More narrowly defined, however, remedial provision is used to refer to relatively short-term provision designed to overcome particular difficulties in an area of the curriculum experienced by individual pupils, with the aim of overcoming that difficulty and moving the pupils on to a point where this remedial provision is no longer necessary. The first usage refers to any pupils who are substantially behind the rest of their age group, while the second implies a notion of under-functioning or under-achievement relative to a child's overall abilities.

For the great majority of children involved, withdrawal for special help certainly does not form the basis of an alternative provision substantially different from the type of education received by their peers in the regular class. For four-fifths of the pupils so withdrawn, withdrawal amounts to, at the most, a little over a tenth of their school experiences and in most cases to rather less. For fewer than one in fifty of children withdrawn for special help does this special provision approach a half of their time in school. The withdrawal timetable of short daily sessions seems modelled on the restricted notion of remedial provision as constituting a little extra help given in areas of specific difficulty, particularly those of reading and writing. Withdrawal time, however, is not in fact used in this restricted way: as mentioned earlier in this chapter, the children with specific reading disability often receive help from the LEA's remedial reading services, and the help through withdrawal is offered to the slowest pupils rather than to pupils who are seen as having specific difficulties relative to their overall ability.

Children with behaviour problems

Although problems associated with behaviour form a substantial proportion of special educational needs in the junior classrooms surveyed, relatively little provision has been made for these difficulties. Of the children described as having behavioural and emotional difficulties, the proportion who are getting special help of any kind – by visits to child guidance clinics, by visits from social workers and through occasional arrangements within a school – amounts to fewer than one in twenty.

Interestingly, in view of the paucity of additional assistance for pupils with behavioural difficulties, the majority of children are not regarded by their teachers as needing such help. In the case of only one child in six described by their teacher as having such difficulties did their teacher also feel that some sort of extra help would be appropriate. About half of these children were felt by their teachers to need child guidance and smaller proportions were felt to need help from psychiatrists, the social services or a variety of other sources. The total number of pupils involved here, both those who are receiving extra help for behavioural difficulties and those for whom their teachers would like such help, amounts to fewer than 20 per cent of the pupils described as having behavioural difficulties. This low figure contrasts dramatically with the proportion of children whose learning difficulties are receiving help: well over half benefit from withdrawal, and only one in five was neither receiving help nor felt by their teacher to require extra help.

Although aware of behavioural and emotional difficulties in their classrooms, junior-school teachers do not, on the whole, feel that there is anything extra which the school ought to be providing to ease these problems. Their attitude probably partly reflects the way in which problems of discipline and classroom control tend to be seen as individual problems with which an individual teacher has to cope, and it may also stem from doubt as to what intervention will be appropriate: the repertoire of remedial techniques available for learning difficulties does not exist for behavioural problems. This view taken by teachers probably also reflects their strong feeling that the majority of behavioural and emotional difficulties are rooted in the home situation of the child and are therefore not amenable to action on the part of the educational system. These issues were dealt with in Chapter 4.

Although there is a substantial minority of the school population who are seen by their teachers as having special educational difficulties because of behavioural or emotional problems or as presenting the school with special difficulties on account of the problems they present with regard to discipline, only a small proportion of these children are seen by their teachers as having special educational needs in the sense that they believe that there is any special provision which it is appropriate to make for them other than the help they may receive if they are also having learning, and particularly reading, difficulties.

The organisation of remedial provision within the school

The provision of remedial help within the junior school is primarily the concern of the individual school and its staff, and individual schools can to a large extent pursue their own policy within the imposed constraints of staffing levels and the availability of other resources. Additional help for children with special needs can be offered in the form of special classes, withdrawal from the classroom for additional help or special assistance provided in the classroom.

(a) Special classes

This type of provision is more 'special' than withdrawal as it means that the children in it will spend most of their school day in this class rather than with the majority of their peers. A special class is not totally separate from the rest of the school, for the children will take part in a range of activities outside their own classroom. Nevertheless, for the largest part of each day they will be in their own small class. It has been argued that special provision of this sort can be very advantageous to some children with learning problems, particularly if they are accompanied by additional behavioural difficulties. On the other hand, this system of provision also has its opponents, principally on the grounds that the regular classroom is the most appropriate place for all or nearly all children.

Of the sixty-one schools in the sample, only three had special classes and these were all in the same authority. These special classes were operated as part of the LEA policy for provision for children with special educational needs. Their operation formed part of the educational service that the head teachers were requested to provide. They were not classes that the head teachers had chosen to operate from within the resources of their schools and there were no instances of special classes being run in this way. Head teachers had mixed views about the desirability of special classes but a substantial majority did not want that sort of provision in their schools. Of the schools who did not have a special class, nearly 64 per cent (63.8 per cent) did not want one. In the case of all but one of these schools the head was against this type of provision on principle.

However, just over 17 per cent (17.2 per cent) of the heads who did not have a special class would have liked to have one but were prevented by lack of resources. Special classes are one of the forms of provision that, for the most part, education authorities leave to the discretion of individual head teachers, yet staffing levels have to be more than usually generous for heads to have any genuine choice in the matter.

(b) Help in the classroom

Children do not necessarily have to leave the classroom and their peers to receive extra help. Special provision can be made in the ordinary classroom for children experiencing the whole range of special needs, not only learning difficulties. The child and his teacher may be helped by having a parent or auxiliary in the classroom or by having more specialist help, such as a remedial or ESL teacher, a teacher for hearing- or visually-impaired children, or occasionally an educational psychologist. In a few schools a head teacher or deputy may also offer extra classroom assistance. Only just over 5 per cent of children with special needs receive this kind of help. This low figure again demonstrates the extent to which it is the class teacher who has to cope with the special needs of the children in her class.

(c) Withdrawal from the regular class

There is no doubting the popularity of withdrawal as a way of meeting special needs. Teachers find it appropriate for a considerable number

Table 8.6 Pupils for whom their teachers would like further withdrawal from the regular class for help with learning difficulties

(More) withdrawal desirable	Pupils already withdrawn		Pupils not currently withdrawn		All pupils with learning difficulties	
	N	%	N	%	N	%
	397	36.5	413	50.9	810	42.7
Total:	1087	100	811	100	1998	100

of children and would like to offer it to many more. As Table 8.6 shows, teachers would like 42.7 per cent of pupils with learning difficulties to receive more extra help outside the classroom than they are receiving at present. In the case of pupils who are currently withdrawn, the teachers would like rather more than a third of them to receive some extra help. This means that, in addition to the 8.8 per cent of the total sample who are currently withdrawn from the regular class for help with learning difficulties, there are a further 3.4 per cent who are not withdrawn but for whom their teachers would like such help.

Head teachers also favour withdrawal. Sixty-four per cent of schools had some sort of withdrawal from the regular class for help with learning problems and the rest would have liked to be able to offer this type of provision. Only 6.5 per cent of heads did not want to have withdrawal procedures in their schools.

All the schools who provide withdrawal offer children extra help specifically with reading. Fifty per cent offer help with number work, though to far fewer children, and 11.8 per cent offer help with all academic work. In addition, 20.6 per cent of heads mentioned withdrawal to assist the child to overcome his behaviour problems, and 14.7 per cent claimed that one reason for offering withdrawal was to remove a disruptive child from the regular classroom.

There are a variety of ways in which children are selected for withdrawal, the most popular being a combination of test results and teacher recommendation: 53.8 per cent of schools employed this system. Test results were the sole basis of selection in 12.8 per cent of schools and teacher recommendation in 30.7 per cent. Teacher assessments of pupils are therefore of crucial importance. Heads thought that teachers based their recommendations on impressions of general performance in the classroom: 48.7 per cent of heads claimed that the staff in their schools made their assessments in this way. The specific skill most frequently mentioned was reading: 20.5 per cent of heads claimed that it was reading performance that was the basis for teacher recommendation. Behaviour as a relevant factor was mentioned by 10.3 per cent of heads but never as the sole factor, since withdrawal is used as a way of offering special help to children with behaviour problems only if they also have learning problems. The specific content of the remedial provision is designed to help learning problems and may as a subsidiary function assist children in overcoming their behaviour problems, but is not primarily intended for this purpose.

Although teacher recommendation is of major importance, 66.6 per cent of schools also use standardised tests as part of the selection procedure. Policy and practice in testing has been dealt with in detail in Chapter 7. Here it can be repeated briefly that the majority of the testing procedures are not particularly well suited to the selection of children with learning difficulties. Only one head used special diagnostic tests to pick out children for special provision.

The remedial teachers

In twenty-four of the thirty-nine schools offering withdrawal to pupils with learning difficulties, this support is provided by a remedial teacher. In one large junior school in an EPA there were two full-time remedial teachers who devoted all their teaching time to this work, but this was a most unusual situation. More typically, the remedial teacher works part-time (fourteen out of the twenty-five remedial teachers interviewed worked part-time) or is a full-time member of the teaching staff who has only part of her teaching commitment devoted to remedial work (this was the situation of six remedial teachers). Altogether, only five of the remedial teachers did this work on a full-time basis. In the schools without a remedial teacher, withdrawal was usually the responsibility of the head or deputy head. With all the other demands that are placed upon the time of teachers in these posts, it is very likely that withdrawal does not take place as regularly as it does when a teacher is appointed specifically for remedial work.

Remedial work may well be done more regularly by a remedial

Table 8.7 Training experience of teachers relating specifically to special educational needs

	Reading	Special needs
Class teachers		
% with any training experience	38.9	20.1
% with relevant initial training experience	17.8	11.7
No. of teachers	428	
Head teachers		
% with any training experience	45.2	31.1
% with relevant initial training experience	3.0	1.6
No. of heads	61	
Remedial teachers		
% with any training experience	38.0	24.0
% with relevant initial training experience	28.0	8.0
No. of remedial teachers	25	

teacher, but it is not at all clear that the work will then be done with greater expertise. Remedial teachers were no more likely than either class or head teachers to have attended any sort of course either on children with special needs or on the teaching of reading. This absence of training is highlighted in the Report by HMI on the effects of local authority expenditure policies on the education service in England, 1982 (DES, July 1983), where it is claimed that, although on the whole there is an improvement in the match between teachers' qualifications and the areas in which they teach, there are still some exceptions (or 'vulnerable subjects'): 'But the pattern of vulnerable subjects and groups of pupils is much as was noted last year with mathematics, science and remedial teaching significantly represented in both primary and secondary schools.' In fact, as is shown in Table 8.7, teachers in general claim that their training in the areas of special educational needs and the teaching of reading is very limited indeed. Only 38.9 per cent of class teachers have had any training specifically in the teaching of reading, which must be regarded as very surprising when the centrality of reading to the primary school curriculum is considered. What training teachers get appears to be provided by part-time in-service courses for practising teachers. It is the head teachers and not the remedial teachers who have (although only marginally) the most training, and this is mainly because they are better attenders at in-service courses. Even so, under half of the heads (45.2 per cent) have had specific training in the teaching of reading

113

and only 31.1 per cent have attended any sort of course relating to special educational needs.

A very high proportion of teachers claim that their initial professional training did not provide them with skills in the teaching of reading. Only 28 per cent of remedial teachers, 17.8 per cent of class teachers and just 3 per cent of head teachers claim that they were taught how to teach children to read. This must surely be regarded as a most serious omission.

It has been pointed out in an earlier chapter that many remedial, as well as class, teachers have a very limited knowledge of the testing of reading. It is difficult to see that remedial teachers, as a group, have particular specialised skills, and their want of expertise may well diminish the effectiveness of withdrawal. This is particularly true as it is the teaching of reading that is the principal task of remedial teachers, and there is a whole range of specialised techniques available to assist teachers in this task if they are aware of them.

All the remedial teachers interviewed said that their withdrawal classes were to assist children with reading problems. Forty-four per cent also helped children who have difficulty with maths, but this help was given on a much more limited scale. The same number claimed that the withdrawal class also functioned, although only secondarily, to assist children who had behaviour problems. This is exactly the position taken by some of the head teachers, who saw withdrawal as a way of helping children who had behaviour problems but only those children who also had reading difficulties. When talking about the beneficial effect that the small withdrawal group had on some children, making them more self-confident and secure, one remedial teacher summed up this position when she said, 'This improvement in behaviour is an effect, but remedial help is not designed to achieve it.' The specific purpose of withdrawal is invariably to help solve learning problems, particularly reading difficulties.

Withdrawal is only rarely offered on an individual basis. In fact, only four children were receiving that kind of help from a remedial teacher. More usually children were taught in small groups, and where possible, pupils with the most acute problems were in groups of between two and six children, and the others in large groups of between seven and twelve children. Sessions of around thirty minutes each, held between three and five times a week, are the most frequently found, though twice-weekly sessions are not unusual. Longer sessions are not so popular, but 16 per cent of remedial teachers held at least some sessions that were over an hour in length. Sessions of this length form a substantial part of the school day, and any child being withdrawn for this length of time may be getting an educational experience substantially different from his peers.

The vast majority (68 per cent) of remedial teachers are satisfied with the materials and resources available to them, and 76 per cent of them are able to hold their classes in a special room. Perhaps it is not surprising that they share the enthusiasm of both class and head teachers for withdrawal of the type they offer, and 72 per cent of them think that more children in the schools where they teach could benefit from this type of help.

The disadvantages of withdrawal

Despite its popularity, withdrawal is seen by many head teachers to have some disadvantages. Forty-one per cent of heads were of the opinion that there were none, but the majority (59 per cent) either found some or else were not sure (4.9 per cent). The heads who elaborated upon the disadvantages mentioned the disruption that withdrawal can cause to a child's learning (16.4 per cent) and the disruption it can cause to the class (4.9 per cent). A further 14.8 per cent thought that taking the child out of the classroom could have a stigmatising effect upon the child that could be harmful. Even though the majority of head teachers thought that withdrawal did have its problems, however, only 8.2 per cent thought that the advantages did not outweigh the disadvantages.

One of the perceived disadvantages of withdrawal is the disruption it can cause to the child's learning and, to a lesser extent, to the whole classroom. Exactly how disruptive the process is will be determined by the length of time a child is absent from the classroom and what he misses while he is withdrawn. The amount of time children spend out of the class is detailed earlier in the chapter. A typical pattern is of several short bursts of thirty minutes or less, spread throughout the week. The total amount of time out of the classroom is usually between one and two hours a week, only a relatively small proportion of the school week.

Probably least disruption is caused if the withdrawn child is pursuing the same activity as his classmates in the regular class, so that a child is withdrawn for extra help with reading when the rest of the class are also reading, or getting help with maths when that is the activity in which his peers are engaged. This is the arrangement in 30.8 per cent of the schools that operate a withdrawal scheme, and it would seem to minimise the possible disadvantages of withdrawal. Disruption to both child and classroom is kept to a minimum, and the child, not missing any of the other activities in his classroom, will not be led to feel markedly different from his classmates. Withdrawal from the classroom at any other time undoubtedly has drawbacks, bringing with it the danger that a few children would have a substantially different experience of school from the majority. In particular it could mean that a child is forced to spend a very long time attempting tasks he cannot do, while at the same time missing out on activities he may be good at and may enjoy. A child who is withdrawn for help with reading when the rest of the class are doing art or project work or maths may well find that a large part of his school day is spent attempting things he cannot master. Meanwhile his skills at other activities are not being developed, so he is slipping behind his peers even in those areas where he may have ability because he is being denied the opportunity to attempt them. This is a serious problem and one that needs consideration by the schools that operate systems of withdrawal.

Overcoming learning difficulties

In examining the nature of the schools' and the teachers' views on the purposes of withdrawal, it is relevant to consider the extent to which they think that children being withdrawn for special help will succeed in overcoming their learning difficulties. Teachers were, therefore, asked to predict the extent to which all pupils whom they had described as having learning difficulties would overcome them. As Table 8.8 shows, the prediction for the great majority of these children was that they would not. Even when children about whose chances the teacher felt unable to speak with any conviction are excluded, well under a third of pupils were thought by their teachers to be likely to overcome their difficulties completely, while in the case of over a fifth of the pupils the teacher thought that the problems would not be overcome at all. The figures are almost identical for children who are being withdrawn for extra help and for children who are not receiving extra provision. These results run counter to one of the original hypotheses

Table 8.8 Teachers' views on the extent to which children will overcome their learning difficulties

Do you think that this child's (learning) problems will be overcome?	Class teachers				Remedial teachers	
	All pupils with learning difficulties		Pupils withdrawn for help		Pupils withdrawn for help	
	No.	%	No.	%	No.	%
Completely	521	27.4	298	27.4	204	40.6
Partly	766	40.4	457	42.0	206	41.0
Not at all	396	20.9	222	20.4	58	11.6
Not sure	215	11.3	110	10.2	32	6.8
Total:	1898	100	1087	100	502	100

of the study, which was that primary teachers will take an optimistic view of the future educational progress of their pupils and will think that most of them would overcome their difficulties in the future. It is interesting to note, however, that remedial teachers are most optimistic about the future progress of children with whom they are dealing. Remedial teachers thought that over 40 per cent of their pupils would completely overcome their learning problems, and in the case of only 11.6 per cent of the children did they think that the problems would not be overcome at all.

Teachers are relatively pessimistic about the future of those of their pupils who have learning difficulties. There can be no doubting the teachers' concern for children with special educational needs: they want to keep the vast majority of these children in ordinary school and they want to offer them assistance, principally within the school by withdrawing them from the regular class for extra help. Yet, in spite of their enthusiasm for this type of provision and their desire to make it more widely available, teachers appear at the same time to expect that their efforts will meet with only limited success.

9 Pupils and teachers in the classroom

A major theme which arises from earlier chapters is that special educational needs form a substantial proportion of the concerns of ordinary schools and teachers. Teachers recognise that up to one in five of the pupils in an average class may have some form of special need, and the provision for such needs is part of the administrative arrangements of all schools. Although classes and schools vary in this respect, few teachers and no schools are free of involvement in special educational needs. It is also clear that, despite the range of out-of-class provision available, special needs are, for the most part, met by class teachers within the context of the ordinary class. As was shown in Chapter 8, of all the pupils described by their teachers as having special educational needs just over half spent any time at all out of the classroom, and, averaged over five days, this amounted to only a small proportion of the school week. For example, just under one in five of all pupils with special needs spent as much as half-an-hour a day out of class, and only about one in forty spent as much as an hour a day out of class.

This makes it clear that, just as teachers are very much aware of the extent of special needs among their pupils, so they also experience these special needs as problems that have to be dealt with in the regular classroom. The pupils who have these special needs spend all or very nearly all of their time in the regular class and share, at least in some respects, the classroom experiences of children who do not have such difficulties. For the most part, therefore, their needs have to be met by class teachers who must try to fit in this aspect of their work alongside the more general demands of classes averaging about thirty pupils.

Two questions in particular arise from this situation. The first concerns the nature of the classroom experiences of pupils with special educational needs and the extent to which these experiences are similar to or differ from those of other pupils. The great majority of pupils with special needs spend most of their time in school alongside other children in the regular class, but it is not clear to what extent they share the classroom experiences of other pupils. This question is also relevant to the issue of greater integration of pupils with relatively severe difficulties into ordinary classrooms. The second question is concerned with how a teacher of a large junior class deals with pupils with special educational needs in that class. This is a question which clearly exercised many of the teachers interviewed as part of the research. As was apparent in Chapter 5, class teachers thought that the regular classroom was the correct educational placement for the great majority of pupils with special educational needs. Nevertheless, many of them commented on the difficulties which these children presented both as requiring more of the teacher's time than could properly be spared and as being perhaps best served by teaching methods that the teacher had not learnt and might not even be identifying accurately. This is reflected in the views expressed by teachers that many of their pupils would benefit from some, or further, withdrawal from the regular class for specialist help. Other research, discussed in the Introduction, suggests that coping with the difficulties of pupils with special needs is an aspect of their work in which teachers are likely to feel particularly ill-equipped by their training.

These two related questions, the nature of the classroom experiences of pupils with special educational needs and the nature of the teacher's relationship with these pupils, are considered in the classroom-focused aspect of the research presented here. As is described in detail in the Appendix, in thirty-four second-year classrooms in two of the local authorities sampled, a programme of testing and systematic observation was carried out in addition to the interviews with class teachers. Some of the results from the reading tests have already been discussed in Chapter 6. In the present chapter, the data presented will be mainly derived from the programme of systematic observation.

The thirty-four second-year junior classrooms studied at this stage in the research were located in twenty junior schools in two local authorities. Class sizes ranged between 17 and 33 with an average of about 29. Thirty-one of the classes had between 25 and 33 pupils. In these classes a total of 280 pupils were observed made up of children with learning problems, children with behaviour problems, children with surprising test scores and a group of control pupils. In this chapter, data will be presented based on observations of 71 pupils described by their teachers as having learning problems, 53 pupils described as having behaviour problems and 129 control pupils. The learning problem and behaviour problem categories are not exclusive, and 27 pupils are included in both groups. This analysis was therefore based on a total of 226 children. Most of the pupils nominated by teachers as having learning or behaviour problems were included in the observation programme: in the case of learning difficulties, 96 pupils were nominated, 12.6 per cent of all the pupils in the classes, and in the case of behaviour problems 68 pupils, 8.9 per cent of all children.

The classroom context: classroom organisation

The overall framework within which pupils experience the primary classroom can be thought of in terms of classroom organisation and curriculum content. Classroom organisation refers to the basic structuring of patterns of interaction between teachers and pupils and between pupils and pupils. Curriculum content refers to the nature of the learning experiences offered to pupils within the classroom. In both these areas there may be a considerable disparity between the experience of classroom life of teachers and of their pupils. This arises both because of the asymmetry between teacher and pupils, a ratio of just under thirty to one in these classes, which necessarily imposes disparities of experience, and also because of the way in which, even in the most tightly regulated classroom, pupils as well as teachers make decisions which influence their experiences.

The organisational background to pupils' classroom experiences is presented in Table 9.1. Whenever a child was a focus of the systematic observation schedule, codes were recorded according to the type of activity he was supposed to be engaged on. The major categories presented in Table 9.1 are: a class lesson (including administrative activities as well as substantive lessons), group work with the teacher, co-operative group work with other pupils but not the teacher, individual work including individual work with the teacher and 'no directed activity', which usually occurred at the beginning or end of teaching sessions. These codes were determined by the context of a child's activities rather than the behaviour he was actually engaged in: a child whispering to a friend during a lecture at the blackboard

Table 9.1 Organisational context of the pupils' experience

	Controls %	Learning problems %	Behaviour problems %
Class lesson (including registration, etc.)	30.3	30.8	30.2
Working in a group with the teacher	3.0	2.5	1.4*
Working co-operatively with other pupils	3.5	2.0	1.7*
Working individually	61.8	63.7	65.8
No directed activity	1.4	1.0	0.9
Total	100	100	100
N =	129	71	53

* Difference from controls statistically significant at the 5 per cent level.

was coded as engaged in a class lesson.

The first column in Table 9.1 shows the organisational context for the control pupils, representing about four-fifths of the children in the classes. The main experience of the classroom for these pupils is of individual work: 61.8 per cent of observations had pupils working individually as their background context. This emphasis on pupils working on their own at individual tasks follows the recommendations of the Plowden Committee on the importance of matching work to individual pupils' needs and confirms the results of other studies of the English junior classroom, such as the ORACLE project (Galton, Simon and Croll, 1980). The next most common experience for pupils is of class work: 30.3 per cent of the observations of the control pupils had as their context a class lesson or administrative activity in which the teacher was interacting with the class as a whole. Working individually and being part of the teacher's class audience accounts for more than nine-tenths of the time the pupils spend in class. Working with the teacher as part of a small group accounts for 3 per cent of the child's time in class and working co-operatively with one or more other pupils accounts for 3.5 per cent of the time.

Two points emerge from this analysis, which we shall return to later. The first is the implications this pattern of classroom organisation has for the difference between the teacher's and the child's experience of the classroom. Less than a third of time in the classroom is spent in interaction between the teacher and the whole class, and yet this is the predominant experience that individual pupils have of interaction with the teacher. As will become apparent when patterns of teacher/pupil interaction are presented, the teacher spends most of her time working with individual pupils on a one-to-one basis. For pupils, however, this can only amount to a small proportion of time in class. The teacher's experience of the classroom is of constant interaction between herself and the children, mainly one at a time. The pupil's experience is mainly of working on his own, and his experience of interaction with the teacher is predominantly as a member of the class audience. These patterns of interaction will be presented in more detail later, but they are implicit in Table 9.1.

The second point to emerge is concerned with grouping and group work. A superficial look at most junior classrooms suggests that grouping is an important organisational principle. Children typically sit in groups around tables or desks placed together; there are often named groups for the purpose of curriculum management. However, the figures in Table 9.1 suggest that these groups are of limited importance with respect to the child's actual experience of the classroom. On only a small proportion of occasions are the children observed either working in a group with the teacher or co-operating with other children on their work or on 'class business' or other administrative activities.

The discussion so far has been concentrated on the control children in order to give an overall view of some organisational features of the classroom and the context within which children's behaviour was observed. The results presented in columns two and three of Table 9.1 show that, for the most part, this analysis holds good for the children with special educational needs as well. With respect to their experience of the basic organisational structure of the classroom, both children with learning difficulties and children with behaviour problems enjoy similar experiences to other pupils, they spend identical levels of time to the control pupils as members of the teacher's class audience and similar levels of time on individual work; in this sense they are part of the class.

The only differences to emerge between the two groups of children with special needs and the control pupils is in the amount of time spent in groups with the teacher and in time spent on co-operative work. Both children with learning difficulties and children with behaviour problems spend less time in these two ways than do control children, and in the case of children with behaviour problems these differences are statistically significant. The converse of this is that these two groups have a proportionally higher level of individual work. Levels of individual activity in all three groups are so high that the differences between the groups are small as a proportion of such activity. But in the case of group and co-operative activity, because the overall levels are low, differences of under 2 per cent nevertheless form a substantial proportion of the total of such experiences.

Lower levels of group work with the teacher for pupils with special needs reflect the patterns of teacher contact with these pupils which will be discussed below. Lower levels of co-operative work may reflect lower levels of ability to sustain such work and possibly reluctance on the part of other children to work co-operatively with children who have behaviour and learning difficulties. Patterns of pupil–pupil interaction for such children will also be discussed below. These differences, although they are relatively large as a proportion of the total of group and co-operative activities, must be seen in the context of the low overall level of such activities. The experiences of those children with special needs and those of other children take place within a similar context of classroom organisation. (A possible source of bias in these comparisons arises from the fact that the control pupils were equally divided between boys and girls while about two-thirds of the children with special needs are boys. In fact, male and female controls had very similar results on the analysis presented here. Details of these results are available from the authors.)

Classroom context: the curriculum

In addition to the organisational context discussed above, the background context to children's activities was also coded in terms of the curriculum content of the activities in which the pupils were supposed to be engaged. Observational procedures for describing the nature of the curriculum experienced by pupils are less well developed than procedures for describing behaviour and interactions within the classroom, and the results reported here, like those of other studies based on systematic observation of classrooms, involve fairly crude and simple categories of curriculum content. (See, for example, Galton, Simon and Croll, 1980.)

Activities were categorised as mathematics, reading (this was coded when reading a book or similar material was the only content of the child's activity) and writing (this was coded when the child was completing any written work except mathematics; it included grammar or spelling exercises, creative writing, writing a report on project work and so on). Other 'literary related' activity was coded if the child was neither doing individual reading nor engaged in writing, but the activity was nevertheless related to literary skills. Activities in this category nearly always occurred during class lessons when the teacher was explaining grammatical rules, extending the children's vocabulary or reading a story. Other non-literary related activities consisted mainly of PE, art and craft, music and so on, but also included some science activities and project work. Non-curriculum activities mainly consisted of 'class business' such as registration and school administration, as well as the organisation of the beginning and end of lessons.

Studies of the values and objectives of teachers such as the Schools Council Aims of Education Project (Ashton et al., 1975) have discredited the recently-fashionable attacks on teachers in Black Papers and similar publications which claimed that teachers had abandoned a commitment to the basic skills, showing instead that literacy and numeracy remain the main academic concern of primary school teachers. The analysis of the curriculum content for control children contained in Table 9.2 shows that the way in which teachers describe their aims is an accurate reflection of the content of classroom activities. The great majority of time in class is spent on curriculum content of some kind; only 6.7 per cent of the time is spent on non-curriculum activities. Mathematics occupies 24.5 per cent of

Table 9.2 *Curriculum content*

	Controls %	Learning problems %	Behaviour problems %
Mathematics	24.5	24.1	24.2
Reading	6.3	7.3	6.0
Writing	31.9	32.7	32.1
Other 'literary related'	8.5	8.7	8.8
Other 'non-literary related'	22.1	22.1	22.4
Non-curriculum activities	6.7	5.1	6.5
Total	100	100	100
N =	129	71	53

time in class, individual reading 6.3 per cent, written work other than mathematics 31.9 per cent and other activities related to literacy 8.5 per cent. Curriculum activities related to neither mathematics nor literacy occupy 22.1 per cent of the time in class. In summary, about a quarter of time in class is spent on mathematics, nearly four-tenths on reading or writing and over seven-tenths on activities related to either mathematics or literacy.

A comparison of the first column of Table 9.2, which shows the content of the curriculum for control pupils, with the second and third columns, which show the curriculum for children with learning difficulties and children with behaviour problems, indicates that the figures for curriculum content are virtually identical for these three groups of children. At least with respect to the very general categories of curriculum content presented in Table 9.2, the classroom experience of children with special educational needs is the same as that of other children. This does not mean that their detailed curriculum experience is the same, but the broad categories of curriculum content presented is identical. As with classroom organisation, the overall context of the classroom is not different for these children from that of the rest of the class.

Classroom activities and behaviour

The overall context of curriculum and organisation within which children experience the classroom is largely within the control of the teacher or the school. However, the particular minute-by-minute activities, interactions and behaviour a child engages in are likely to reflect characteristics of individual pupils as well as characteristics of the overall classroom setting. The measures of classroom context discussed above form the background to the child's experience in class. In addition to these, at every ten seconds during the period of observation the child being observed was coded according to the kind of activity he was engaged in, the kind of interactions he was engaged in and whether he was moving around the classroom, sitting (or occasionally standing) still or fidgeting.

In this way it is possible to compare some of the patterns of behaviour and interaction in the classroom of children who have special educational needs with the behaviour and interactions of the control pupils. In the pilot study for the present research it was suggested that there is a distinctive pattern of classroom behaviour characteristic of children with learning difficulties, a 'slow learner behaviour pattern' (Moses, 1982). This behaviour pattern is characterised by children spending less time engaged on their work than other children and, conversely, more time distracted. This time distracted from work is typically spent alone rather than in interaction with other pupils, and such children are also characterised by high levels of fidgeting. There is further reason to expect that children with behaviour problems will exhibit distinctive behavioural characteristics, partly because many such children also have learning difficulties but also because this seems implicit in the nature of the problem.

In Table 9.3 a number of categories of pupil activities in class are presented. Pupils were categorised as: working directly on their curriculum task, working on activities relevant to that task (fetching or preparing materials, waiting to see the teacher, etc.), distracted from their task (but not involved in aggressive activities), involved in aggression towards other pupils, involved in aggression towards property, involved in class business (registration, listening to administrative announcements), engaged in a disciplinary interaction (being 'told off' individually or collectively), and a small category of other activities which mainly occurred during an organisational

Table 9.3 Pupil activities in class

	Controls %	Learning problems %	Behaviour problems %
Working on curricular task	57.0	50.5*	48.8*
Working on task-related activity	19.4	18.5	17.0*
Distracted from work	17.2	25.1*	27.4*
Aggression to other pupils	0.1	0.2*	0.3*
Aggression to property	0.1	0.2*	0.3*
Involved in class business	2.9	2.4	2.7
Disciplinary interaction	0.6	0.8*	1.3*
Other	2.7	2.2	2.2
Total	100	100	100
Mobile	6.1	6.6	6.8
Fidgeting	5.9	11.3*	11.1*
N =	129	71	53

* Difference from controls statistically significant at 5 per cent level.

126

context of 'no directed activity', when there was no activity on which the child was supposed to be engaged.

In Table 9.3 it can be seen that the control children, representing the majority of children in the class, are applying themselves to approved, curricular-related activities for the greater part of their time in class. The classrooms in this study are principally characterised by high levels of involvement by both pupils and teachers and low levels of misbehaviour or other non-approved activities. Fifty-seven per cent of the control children's class time is spent working directly on a curriculum task and a further 19.4 per cent on activities related to such tasks. Activities involving aggressive behaviour to other pupils and to property each take up 0.1 per cent of observations, and most of these are of a fairly minor kind. The total of time distracted from an approved activity is 17.4 per cent. The children are also usually at their places: 6.1 per cent of observations were of children who were moving around the classroom, and on a further 5.9 per cent of observations pupils were fidgeting. This picture of the classroom as orderly and industrious also emerges from the other major obser-vational study of junior classes, the ORACLE programme of research (Galton, Simon and Croll, 1980).

The categories in Table 9.3 describe the activities the children were actually engaged in, rather than the context for these activities as in Tables 9.1 and 9.2. It might therefore be expected that there will be differences between the children with special educational needs and the control children, and columns two and three of Table 9.3 show that this is the case. Both the children with learning difficulties and children with behaviour problems spend less time engaged on approved activities than do the control pupils. This difference is particularly evident for time spent directly on a curriculum task. Time spent on class business and on work-related activities are only a little below the level of control children, but time spent directly on a task is 50.5 per cent for the children with learning difficulties and 48.8 per cent for children with behaviour problems; in both cases this difference is statistically significant. The time that the two groups of children with special needs spend in aggressive activities is higher than that of the control pupils, reaching a total of 0.6 per cent in the case of children with behaviour problems, and the total amount of time these two groups spend distracted from approved activities is half as much again as that of the control pupils. This distraction from approved activity also makes heavy inroads on the time the children

127

spend directly on curriculum tasks.

One of the features of the 'slow learner behaviour pattern' outlined by Moses (1982) was that these children spend higher than average amounts of time fidgeting; tapping the desk with a foot, fiddling with pencils or rulers, swinging about on their chairs and similar behaviour. The bottom row of Table 9.3 shows that this is true both of the group of children with learning difficulties and of those with behaviour problems. Both these groups had levels of fidgeting virtually double that of control pupils. These two groups were not, however, more likely to move around the classroom than other children: like the control children they spend well over nine-tenths of their time in class stationary.

Teacher–pupil interaction

The asymmetry between the teachers' and the pupils' experiences of the classroom, particularly as this relates to teacher–pupil interaction, is indicated by the figures for teacher–pupil interaction presented in Table 9.4. The average control child spends 22.9 per cent of his time in the classroom as part of the teacher's whole-class audience and a further 2.4 per cent as part of a small group interacting with the

Table 9.4 Teacher–pupil interaction

	Controls %	Learning problems %	Behaviour problems %
Class audience	22.9	20.9	19.3
Group audience	2.4	2.1	1.3*
Individual attention	1.9	3.3*	3.2*
Individual attention – class context	0.3	0.4	0.5*
Individual attention – group context	0.3	0.4	0.5*
Total individual contact	2.5 (63% on task)	4.1* (63.5% on task)	4.1* (56.7% on task)
Total teacher contact	27.8	27.1	24.7
N =	129	71	53

* Difference from controls statistically significant at 5 per cent level.

teacher. Time spent privately with the teacher accounts for 1.9 per cent of the child's time in class. A further 0.3 per cent is spent as the focus of the teacher's attention in a class context (e.g. answering or being asked a question during a class lesson) and the same amount of time is spent in similar interaction during group lessons. Although 27.8 per cent of time is spent in some form of interaction with the teacher, only 2.5 per cent is spent as the main focus of the teacher's interaction. In contrast, as will be shown when interactions are analysed from the teacher's point of view, teachers spend nearly all their time interacting with children, and most of this interaction is on an individual basis. (The difference between the amount of class interaction here and in Table 9.1 is accounted for by the fact that these figures refer to a child's actual interactions rather than their context. A child can be distracted from a class lesson, and during the context of a class lesson there may be no teacher–pupil interaction, as when children are copying passages from the board or privately writing down their answers.)

The main difference between the control pupils and the two groups of children with special educational needs in their patterns of teacher interaction lies in the amount of individual attention they receive from the teacher. Children with learning difficulties receive private individual attention for 3.3 per cent of the time and children with behaviour problems for 3.2 per cent of the time, compared with 1.9 per cent for the controls. If all individual attention is included both these figures rise to 4.1 per cent, contrasted with 2.5 per cent for controls.

Clearly, the teacher's experience of pupils with special needs in the classroom involves their occupying more of her time than do other pupils. Although the absolute amount of time available for these children on an individual basis is still fairly small they receive considerably more time than other pupils do. It is also noticeable that this extra individual attention does not arise simply from a necessity for higher levels of disciplinary interaction with these pupils or for more lengthy administrative and organisational procedures. In the case of children with learning difficulties the proportion of individualised teacher interactions directly concerned with the content of work is identical to that of the control children. In the case of children with behaviour problems this proportion is rather lower, reflecting the problems of discipline and control which these children present, but the difference is not nearly as great as the difference between the

129

totals of individual interactions. The behaviour problems are still receiving a higher level of work-oriented interactions than the controls.

This higher level of individual attention to children with special educational needs is achieved both by higher levels of private interaction and also by the teacher's picking these children out during class and group lessons. However, the total of class and group interactions with the two groups of children, and particularly of the behaviour problems, is below that of controls, and this results in the children with behaviour problems having rather lower levels of overall teacher interaction. Their slightly lower interaction as members of a class audience is due to the fact that these pupils pay less attention during such lessons, as the identical levels of 'class context' shown in Table 9.1 demonstrates. The lower level of actual group interaction is paralleled, however, by lower levels of 'group context' in Table 9.1, and this suggests a somewhat different approach by the teacher to interaction with these pupils. The teachers' higher levels of individual interaction with children who have behaviour problems, and possibly to some extent with those who have learning difficulties, accompany lower levels of interaction with them as members of a group.

Pupil–pupil interaction

Another aspect of the pupils' classroom experience is the type of level and interaction with other children in the class. Most of a pupil's time in class is occupied by interaction not with the teacher but with other pupils, interactions that are social in character or concerned with work and work-related activities. In Table 9.5 the amounts of time spent by pupils in these sorts of interaction are presented. In the case of control pupils 19 per cent of time in class is spent in interaction with other pupils, and of this nearly three-quarters is spent interacting with one other child rather than with a group of children. This interaction is fairly evenly divided between interactions which are a distraction from the activities on which the pupils are supposed to be engaged and interactions which form part of approved activities, such as working on a joint task.

The total level of pupil–pupil interaction for the children with special educational needs is very similar to that of control children. Children with learning difficulties are interacting with other children

Table 9.5 Pupil–pupil interaction

	Controls %	Learning problems %	Behaviour problems %
(a)			
Interaction with one other pupil	13.9	13.4	14.8
Interaction with group	5.1	4.0	4.3
Total pupil–pupil interaction	19.0	17.5	19.2
N =	129	71	53
(b)			
Interaction directly on task	4.3	3.2*	2.6*
Interaction related to work or class business	4.6	3.2*	3.2*
Interaction distracted from work	9.2	10.3	12.5*
Other interaction	0.9	0.8	0.9
Total pupil–pupil interaction	19.0	17.5	19.2
N =	129	71	53

* Difference from controls statistically significant at 5 per cent level.

for 17.5 per cent of the school day and children with behaviour problems for 19.2 per cent, compared with 19 per cent for the controls. However, the two groups of children with special needs are less likely than other children to be involved with other pupils in work or other approved activities, and a greater proportion of their time spent with other children is a distraction from work. Nevertheless, especially in the case of the children with learning difficulties, the total of 'distracting' interaction is only slightly above that of the controls, 10.3 per cent compared with 9.2 per cent. Children with behaviour problems have a rather higher level of 12.5 per cent of time engaged in 'distracting' interaction.

Alone in class

It is evident from the figures for teacher–pupil interaction and pupil–pupil interaction that, on average, over half a child's class time is spent not interacting. The figures in Table 9.6 show that the average control child spends 53.1 per cent of time in class on his own in the sense that he is not interacting either with the teacher or with any of his fellow pupils. The figures for children with learning problems and

Table 9.6 Time spent not interacting

	Controls %	Learning problems %	Behaviour problems %
Time spent not interacting	53.1	55.2	56.0
Time spent not interacting and distracted	7.8	14.5*	14.6*
N =	129	71	53

* Difference from controls statistically significant at 5 per cent level.

children with behaviour problems are slightly higher at 55.2 per cent and 56 per cent respectively. The difference between these two groups of pupils and the controls becomes much more dramatic, however, when the amounts of time spent alone, distracted from work, are compared. The amount of time the pupils with special needs spend in this way is almost double that of the controls. Control pupils spend 7.8 per cent of their time in class not interacting and not working or engaged in other approved activities: children with learning difficulties spend 14.5 per cent of their time in this way, and children with behaviour problems 14.6 per cent. These differences from the control pupils in the amount of time engaged in solitary distractions are much greater than the differences in the amounts of time spent distracted from work in interaction with other pupils.

Summary: the classroom experience of pupils with special educational needs

The analysis above has compared the classroom experience of two overlapping groups of pupils identified by their teachers as having special educational needs, namely, children with learning difficulties and children with behaviour problems, with a sample of control pupils. The overall classroom context in terms of the framework of class organisation and curriculum content was very similar for the different groups of pupils. In terms of the framework provided by the teacher, the children with special needs were part of the ordinary class. An exception to this is found in the relatively lower amount of time the children with special needs spent in the context of group instruction with the teacher and work involving co-operation with other pupils, but these activities form only a small part of the average child's classroom experiences.

In terms of their behaviour and interactions in class, however, a number of differences emerged between the two groups of special needs children and the rest of the pupils in the class. The first of these is that both groups of special needs children spent a good deal less time than the other pupils engaged in work and other approved activities and, conversely, more time distracted from approved tasks. This difference is greatest in the case of work directly on a curriculum task. The children in the two special needs groups had higher levels of aggressive behaviour than control pupils, although overall levels of such behaviour were low, and also spent a great deal more of their time than control pupils fidgeting. They were not, however, more likely to move around the classroom.

Teachers spend more time on an individual basis with the children with special needs than with other pupils although this is necessarily only a small part of the child's classroom experience. Levels of interaction with other pupils on the part of children with special needs is very similar to that of the control sample, although it is rather less likely to be concerned with work and other approved activities. However, interaction with other pupils even as a distraction from work is only a little higher among the two groups of special needs pupils. Where they differ considerably from the control pupils is in distraction from work which does not involve interaction with other pupils. This solitary distraction from work is about double that of the control pupils.

The results presented here confirm Moses's hypothesis that there is a distinctive set of behavioural characteristics among children with learning difficulties, a 'slow learner behaviour pattern'. This involves lower levels of engagement in work, particularly work directly on a curriculum task, high levels of fidgeting and much more time than other children spent on their own, distracted from their work. Teachers spend considerably more time with these children on an individual basis than they do with other pupils but, like the rest of the class, the children with learning difficulties have most experience of interaction with the teacher as part of a class audience. The children with behaviour problems share most of the characteristics of children with learning difficulties (and half of them are also in the learning difficulties group). Differences include teachers being rather less likely to work with them as members of a small group and a higher level of distraction from work in interaction with other pupils than is found among the children with learning difficulties.

Some of these results suggest, by implication, the difficulties that teachers may have with children who have learning difficulties and behaviour problems, particularly in finding ways of engaging them in their work. This should be put in context, however. Although their children do less work than most pupils they are still directly engaged on curriculum tasks for, on average, about half of their time in class and spend about seven-tenths of their time on some sort of approved activity. They are fidgeting but not constantly moving about the class, and aggressive behaviour, although higher than among the controls, is still very low. Interaction with other children in the class is the same as that of the control pupils, and the children with learning difficulties are not above average in engaging in distracting interaction with others. They do, though, take up more of the teacher's time than other pupils, and their levels of solitary distraction from their work suggest that this extra attention cannot be sufficient to engage them in their work to the extent achieved by most children.

10 Other aspects of classroom behaviour and special educational needs

The preceding chapter gave an outline account of the classroom behaviour and interactions of pupils regarded by their teachers as having special educational needs and contrasted these with the behaviour and interactions of other pupils in the class. This chapter considers three further aspects of the classroom experiences and relationships with teachers of pupils with special educational needs. The first section looks in more detail at pupils with different types of difficulty to see whether there are differences in the classroom experiences and behaviour of children with different kinds of learning and behaviour difficulty. The second section compares the involvement in work of pupils with special needs and control pupils across different sorts of classroom context in order to see whether different settings influence differential levels of work engagement. The third section takes up the question of the relationship between the classroom behaviour of pupils and the assessments made of them by their teachers and considers, in particular, the possible influence exerted by a child's pattern of behaviour upon the teacher's assessment of that child's level of achievement.

Different types of learning and behaviour problems

The analysis presented in Chapter 9 showed the patterns of classroom behaviour of pupils who had been described by their teachers as having either learning problems or behaviour problems. These overall categories accurately reflect the types of special educational need most prevalent in junior classrooms but also contain within them more detailed differentiation of children's difficulties. By far the most frequent terms used by teachers to describe children with learning problems were 'poor reader' and 'slow learner'. Usually these expressions were applied to the same child: the child's reading difficulties were seen as part of an overall pattern of slow learning. However, some children were regarded as having specific reading problems. They were described as 'poor readers' but not as having all-round learning difficulties. There were also children described by their teachers as 'slow learners' but whose difficulties did not include problems with reading. Of the seventy-one children with learning difficulties of any kind who were the subjects of observation, eight were poor readers but not slow learners and ten were slow learners but not poor readers.

Further distinctions can also be made among the fifty-three children described as behaviour problems. Of these pupils, twenty-six were described as having behaviour problems but not presenting the teacher with a discipline problem, while twenty-seven were both behaviour problems and discipline problems. Another way of dividing up these pupils is to distinguish between those children who have behaviour problems in addition to learning difficulties and those who have behaviour problems without also having learning difficulties. The first group consists of twenty-six children and the second of twenty-seven.

The analysis presented in the previous chapter showed that on a number of measures of classroom behaviour and interaction children with special needs differed from other pupils in the class. Generally speaking, the two major groups of children with special needs, pupils with learning difficulties and pupils with behaviour problems, had similar behaviour patterns which differed in certain respects from those of the control pupils. These children were less likely to be involved in approved classroom activities than other children and were in particular less likely to be engaged directly on a curriculum task. They fidgeted more than other pupils and were more likely to be distracted from work but did not have higher levels of pupil–pupil interaction, and their higher level of time distracted was mainly characterised by solitary distraction from work. The children with special needs also received more individual attention from the teacher than did other pupils. It is these categories of behaviour and inter-action that are presented in Tables 10.1 and 10.2, where a more detailed differentiation of pupils with special educational needs is shown. The categories presented in these tables are a selection from the total of activities observed: they do not cover the full range of activities and are not mutually exclusive.

Table 10.1 Classroom behaviour and different types of learning problem

	Slow learners/ poor readers %	Slow learners/ not poor readers %	Poor readers/ not slow learners %
Work	49.1	50.3	60.3*
All approved activities	70.1	69.5	82.6*
Fidgeting	11.2	15.2	7.3
Individual teacher attention	3.9	4.8	4.4
Pupil interaction	18.7	15.5	11.7*
Distracted alone	15.0	16.6	8.5*
Distracted together	11.1	9.0	6.6*
N =	53	10	8

* Difference between poor readers and the other two groups combined statistically significant at the 5 per cent level.

In Table 10.1 pupils who have been described as slow learners but not as poor readers and pupils who have been described as poor readers but not as slow learners are compared with the much larger group of pupils who have been described as both. In the pilot study for the present research, where it was first suggested that there is a distinct 'slow learner behaviour pattern', it was also suggested that children with specific reading difficulties have patterns of classroom behaviour rather different from those of pupils with all-round learning difficulties (Moses, 1982). The figures presented in Table 10.1 lend support to this conclusion. The largest group of pupils, those who are described both as slow learners and as poor readers, have patterns of behaviour very similar to those of the whole group of children with learning difficulties who were discussed in the previous chapter. This is inevitable as they make up over three-quarters of this group. The group of children described as slow learners but not poor readers are generally similar to the slow learner/poor reader group although they have rather higher levels of fidgeting and rather lower levels of interaction with other pupils. The children with specific reading difficulties, however, differ substantially from the other children with learning difficulties and cannot be said to form part of the slow learner behaviour pattern. Their level of involvement in curriculum tasks is very much higher than that of other pupils with learning difficulties, as is their involvement in all approved activities. These figures for curriculum tasks and approved activities of 60.3 per cent and 82.6 per cent are not only significantly different from those of the other learning difficulties pupils but are even slightly above the figures for control pupils. In other respects, such as fidgeting and the amount of time they spend distracted on their own, these poor readers are again much more like the control pupils than they are like other children with learning difficulties. Their levels of interaction with other pupils, though, are much lower than those of the controls and of other children with learning difficulties, as are the levels of time these children spend distracted from their work in interaction with others. This analysis shows that the slow learner behaviour pattern does not apply to all children with learning difficulties and that children with specific reading problems have patterns of classroom behaviour more typical of the control pupils. Where they differ from the control pupils is in their low levels of pupil–pupil interaction, an area of classroom behaviour in which control pupils and other pupils with learning difficulties are similar. Poor readers are similar to slow learning pupils, however, in having higher levels of individual teacher attention than the controls, and though the absolute numbers of poor readers is small the differences reach statistical significance.

Further distinctions can also be made in the case of pupils with behaviour problems. In the description they gave of their pupils, teachers said that some pupils had behaviour problems which presented problems of classroom discipline while other pupils had behaviour problems which did not result in discipline problems. Some aspects of the classroom behaviour of these two groups of pupils are presented in Table 10.2.

Table 10.2 *Classroom behaviour and different types of behaviour problems*

	Controls %￼	All behaviour problems %	Behaviour alone %	Behaviour and discipline %
Work on curriculum task	57.0	48.8	49.9	47.7
All approved activities	79.4	68.5	69.7	67.4
Fidgeting	5.9	11.1	10.6	11.5
Individual teacher attention	2.5	4.1	3.6	4.5
Pupil interaction	19.0	19.2	17.7	20.6
Distracted alone	7.8	14.6	14.6	14.6
Distracted with others	9.2	12.5	11.7	13.4
N =	129	53	26	27

The figures in Table 10.2 show that children who are discipline problems and children who have behaviour problems which do not present discipline problems have similar types and levels of classroom activity and interaction, as they have been measured in the present research. On the variables presented in Table 10.2, the discipline problems children present a slightly more extreme version of the levels of the other behaviour problem children but nevertheless form part of the overall behaviour pattern. They have slightly lower levels of work involvement and slightly higher levels of distraction and fidgeting, but the two groups are similar to one another and to the children with learning difficulties and differ from the control pupils.

A further aspect of a more detailed discussion of the patterns of classroom activities and interactions of children with different sorts of special educational need arises from the overlap in membership of the two major groups of special needs, namely learning difficulties and behaviour problems. The analysis in the previous chapter showed that children with learning difficulties have a pattern of classroom behaviour, common also to children with behaviour problems, which distinguishes both groups from the control pupils. A complication arises because of the overlap in group membership. Half of the pupils described as having behaviour problems are also described as having learning difficulties, and this group of pupils with both sorts of difficulty makes up over a third of the pupils with learning difficulties. Consequently, there is a possibility that the apparent similarity of behaviour between the two groups arises because of the extent of joint group-membership and not because of similar behavioural charac-teristics among pupils experiencing the two categories of difficulty. Such an explanation might mean that children with behaviour problems alone will not have similar behaviour patterns to the children with learning difficulties. Alternatively, it could mean that there is not a 'slow learner behaviour pattern' at all, but a 'behaviour problem behavior pattern' which the behaviour problems among the slow learners share.

The analysis to investigate these possibilities is presented in Table 10.3. Values for those aspects of classroom behaviour which are of particular interest in delineating the distinctive pattern of behaviour for pupils with special educational needs are presented for the two overlapping groups of pupils with learning difficulties and pupils with behaviour problems and also for pupils with learning difficulties alone, for pupils with behaviour problems alone and for pupils with

Table 10.3 Classroom behaviour, learning difficulties and behaviour problems

	Controls	All learning difficulties	Learning difficulties alone	Learning difficulties/ behaviour problems	Behaviour problems alone	All behaviour problems
	%	%	%	%	%	%
Work on curriculum task	57.0	50.5	53.6*	45.5	52.2*	48.8
All approved activities	79.4	71.5	75.4*†	65.1	72.1*†	18.5
Fidgeting	5.9	11.3	10.3†	12.8	9.2†	11.1
Individual teacher attention	2.5	4.1	3.9†	4.3	3.8†	4.1
Pupil interaction	19.0	17.5	16.2	19.5	18.8	19.2
Distracted alone	7.8	14.5	12.9*†	17.0	12.2*†	14.6
Distracted with others	9.2	10.3	8.5*	13.2	11.8	12.5
N =	129	71	44	27	26	53

* Difference from learning difficulties/behaviour problems group statistically significant.

† Difference from controls statistically significant at the 5 per cent level.

both learning difficulties and behaviour problems. Values for the control pupils are also given. Significance tests of two sorts have been performed on the figures in this table. The two groups of pupils with either only behaviour problems or only learning difficulties are compared with the control pupils and are also compared with the pupils who have both learning difficulties and behaviour problems.

The main point to arise from Table 10.3 is that when pupils with both kinds of special need are removed from the analysis the two remaining groups of pupils with special needs, that is, pupils with learning difficulties only and pupils with behaviour problems only, retain behavioural characteristics in the classroom distinctive to them and differing from those of the control pupils. However, when the pupils with both sorts of difficulty are removed from the analysis the difference between children with special needs and the controls is reduced. Both the children with learning difficulties alone and the pupils with behaviour problems alone differ from the controls in spending less time on curriculum tasks, less time on all approved activities, more time fidgeting and more time distracted on their own, but these differences are in all cases less than those occurring in the original analysis, and the differences in time spent directly on a curriculum task are no longer statistically significant. It is not the case that the patterns of behaviour associated with learning difficulties and behaviour problems which were described in the previous chapter are really only associated with one of these types of difficulty. The extent, however, of the difference between pupils with either of these difficulties alone and the control pupils is smaller than it appeared when children with both sorts of difficulty were included in the analysis.

It follows from the above that the association of the two sorts of difficulty with a distinctive pattern of behaviour must be cumulative and that pupils characterised as having learning difficulties and behaviour problems will exhibit a more extreme version of the behaviour pattern. This is shown to be the case in Table 10.3. The figures for children with both behaviour and learning difficulties are further removed from those of the control pupils than are those of the other children. The children with both sorts of difficulty spend 45.5 per cent of their time on curriculum tasks and 65.1 per cent on all approved activities compared with values of 57 per cent and 79.4 per cent for the controls. They spend 12.8 per cent of their time fidgeting, 17 per cent distracted on their own and 13.2 per cent distracted in interaction with others compared with 5.9 per cent, 7.8 per cent and 9.2 per cent for the controls. Their values for time spent on curriculum tasks, time on approved activities, and time spent distracted on their own are significantly different from those of the pupils with either learning difficulties or behaviour difficulties alone. Pupils with only one sort of difficulty have a behaviour pattern different from the controls, and the children with both kinds of difficulty show a more exaggerated version of this pattern. It is worth noting that the difference is proportionately greater in the amount of time they spend distracted on their own, over a sixth of the time spent in class by these children. Differences in the amount of time they spend distracted together with other pupils are considerably smaller, and the amount of time spent altogether in pupil–pupil interaction is remarkably similar for the various groups of children with special needs and for the control children.

Although the pupils with both sorts of difficulty show more extreme values for most of the distinctive characteristics of pupils with special needs, this is so only to a very slight extent in the case of individual

141

teacher attention. Children with special needs generally receive considerably higher levels of individual attention than do the control pupils, but these levels are similar for all the different categories of children with special needs.

Contexts of work involvement

From the previous analyses it is clear that a major problem for teachers in dealing with the special educational needs of their pupils is the lower level of engagement in school work which is characteristic both of children with learning difficulties and of those with behaviour problems. It is therefore interesting to consider the different extent of different types of pupils' work engagement in different types of organisational context.

It was shown in the previous chapter that individual work was the predominant form of organisation of pupils' activities, occupying over 60 per cent of pupils' time, in the classrooms observed. Class work was the next most common type of experience, occupying about half this amount of time, and working in a small group with a teacher was a relatively infrequent type of experience for pupils, occupying only about 3 per cent of class time. In Table 10.4 the extent of work involvement during these kinds of activities is compared for three kinds of pupils. The control children are compared with children described as slow learners and with children described as behaviour problems but who did not also have learning difficulties. Children with specific reading difficulties have been excluded from the analysis as they do not have low levels of engagement in work, and children

Table 10.4 *Context of work involvement*

Proportion of time spent on curriculum task during:	Controls	Slow learners	Behaviour problems only
	%	%	%
Class work	59.4	55.0	55.5
Group work with teacher	62.2	71.1*	76.9*
Individual work	57.0	46.2*	50.4*
N =	129	63	26

* Differences from controls statistically significant at the 5 per cent level.

with behaviour problems alone are shown separately in order to avoid the sorts of complication discussed in the previous section.

The figures in Table 10.4 show some variation in the level of the control pupils' engagement in work during different types of activity. The level of involvement is highest when children are working in a small group with the teacher: involvement directly on a curriculum task is 62.2 per cent. It is at its lowest during individual work, when it is 57 per cent, and class work falls in between these with a level of 59.4 per cent. (These figures average at slightly higher than the overall curriculum-engagement figures used earlier because periods of 'no directed activity', which rarely involve curriculum work, have been excluded.) These differences in the level of involvement experienced in different sorts of activities also occur for the slow-learning children and for the children with behaviour problems. Engagement in work is highest during group work and lowest during individual work for all three groups of children. What is particularly interesting, however, is that although the overall pattern for the three groups is the same, the extent of the differences is very much greater for the two groups of children with special educational needs. In the case of control pupils, involvement in work varies from 62.2 per cent during group work to 57 per cent during individual work with a value of 59.4 per cent for class work. But in the case of slow-learning pupils the variation is from 71.1 per cent during group work to 46.2 per cent during individual work, with a value of 55 per cent during class work. Similarly, the behaviour problem children vary from 76.9 per cent during group work to 50.4 per cent during individual work, with a value of 55.5 per cent during class work. While the type of work organisation is associated with only small differences in levels of engagement for the majority of children in the class, for slow learning children and children with behaviour problems whose overall level of engagement is below average, the type of work organisation is associated with considerable differences in involvement.

It should be noted that the category of group work with the teacher does not necessarily mean the same for the three groups of pupils. Teachers may construct groups of different sizes or compositions or use them during different sorts of activity for children with special needs, whose experience of group work might therefore differ from the rest of the class, and the higher levels of work engagement on the part of the children with special needs during group work must be seen in the context of these possible differences. What is clear, however, is that during the times when children are working individually many children with special needs, and especially slow-learning children, are particularly likely to have low levels of involvement. It has already been shown that individual work is the predominant pattern of work organisation in the classrooms observed in the present study. During individual work teachers spend more time with the children who have special needs than with other pupils, but this is necessarily only a small part of the time pupils spend working alone and it is evidently not enough to bring these pupils' levels of work involvement up to average. Time spent in small groups with the teacher, by contrast, is particularly likely to secure an increase in these children's work involvement. However, not only is this a relatively infrequent type of work organisation but it is also the type of organisation, as was shown in the previous chapter, which children with special needs are less likely than other pupils to experience.

Teacher assessments and classroom behaviour

The results presented above generally provide support for the hypothesis that there are distinctive patterns of classroom behaviour among children with various sorts of special educational need. It was further suggested in the pilot study that these behaviour patterns might sometimes mislead teachers in their assessments. Although the behaviour patterns are associated with particular sorts of difficulty, this association is by no means a perfect one. In particular it was hypothesised that a child who was struggling academically but whose classroom behaviour was not typical of a slow learner would be less likely to be identified by a teacher than one who matched the slow learner behaviour pattern and that a child whose behaviour was typical of a slow learner might be regarded as such even if his achievements were average.

Moses (1982) suggested that these results in the pilot study were probably connected with the absence of systematic testing in the classes used in the research. The classes in the present study did use reading tests, and so it may be that behaviour is less likely to influence assessments than had been hypothesised. Moreover, it is clear that teachers have identified a group of children as poor readers despite patterns of behaviour more typical of control pupils.

In Table 10.5 three groups of children whose test results surprised their teachers are compared with the control pupils and with pupils who have learning difficulties. There were eight children who surprised the teacher by their low score on the reading tests. These pupils had average scores of about twenty months behind their chronological age. The hypothesis that behaviour influenced this assessment would suggest that these children's behaviour patterns were like the control pupils' rather than like those of children with learning difficulties. This turns out to be the case. On the separate counts of total time at work, work on curricular tasks, total distracted time, time distracted alone and fidgeting, these pupils had levels more like those of control children than of the children with learning difficulties. This does not necessarily mean, however, that the teachers' assessments have been influenced by the children's behaviour. It could also be that the teachers' original views of the pupils are correct and that the tests have failed to reflect these children's reading achievements.

The next two groups whose scores surprised their teachers consist of pupils who gained higher scores and pupils who gained lower

Table 10.5 *Classroom behaviour and teacher assessments*

Classroom behaviour	Controls %	Learning problems %	Results which surprise teacher		
			High NVR %	Low NVR %	Low RA %
Work on curricular activities	57.0	50.5	51.4	61.3	56.2
Work-related, class business, etc.	22.4	21.0	23.5	20.5	21.5
Total work-related activity	79.0	71.5	74.9	81.8	77.7
Distracted alone	7.8	14.4	12.5	7.3	9.0
Distracted in interaction with others	9.2	10.3	8.8	8.1	9.5
Aggression to other pupils	0.1	0.2	0.1	0.1	0.4
Aggression to property	0.1	0.2	0.1	0.03	0.04
Other distraction	0.1	0.4	0.3	0.2	0.4
Total distracted activity	17.3	25.5	21.9	15.7	19.3
Total interaction with other pupils	19.0	17.5	17.9	16.8	17.2
Fidgeting	5.9	11.3	8.0	5.9	5.4
Moving around classroom	6.1	6.6	6.8	5.2	5.4
N =	129	71	16	22	8

scores than expected on tests of non-verbal reasoning. It is clear from the figures in Table 10.5 that the children who did surprisingly well in these tests had similar behaviour patterns to the children with learning difficulties, while the children with surprisingly poor scores had similar patterns to the controls. For surprisingly low scorers this pattern occurs with respect to all the variables. For surprisingly high scorers it is clearest with respect to time on curriculum tasks and time spent distracted alone, but also holds to a lesser extent for total time on work-related activity, time distracted and fidgeting.

These results do not mean that the classroom behaviour of pupils is misleading their teachers in the assessment of their achievements. The tests of non-verbal reasoning do not measure achievement in class, and the results are not incompatible with the teachers' having correctly assessed their actual classroom performance. In fact the surprisingly low scorers had reading ages nearly ten months on average ahead of their chronological age. The surprisingly high scorers were on average nearly two months behind.

Nevertheless, the results do suggest that there are aspects of children's abilities of which teachers are less aware than they are, for example, of reading skills, and it is noteworthy that there were many more surprising non-verbal reasoning scores than reading scores. The children who surprised their teachers by an unexpectedly high level of performance on the test of non-verbal reasoning are a group of pupils with moderate reading difficulties and possibly low levels of all-round achievement. The fact that they have behaviour patterns typical of slow-learning children may partly account for their teachers' unawareness of abilities they possess.

11   Summary and implications

The first, and in some ways most important, finding to come out of this study is that the incidence of special educational needs in junior classes as estimated by junior-school teachers matches the estimate contained in the Warnock Report that between one in five and one in six children have special educational needs. This suggests that there is a sufficient degree of consensus about the applicability of the broad concept of special educational needs to provide a basis for the major contribution which it is hoped that teachers in ordinary schools will make in this area. Teachers recognise the special needs of a substantial minority of their pupils and see them, for the most part, as being the responsibility of the ordinary school.

That these special needs are essentially of an educational kind is indicated by the way in which learning difficulties dominate the teachers' perspectives. About four-fifths of the children identified by their teachers had learning difficulties, sometimes together with other problems. The most commonly identified learning difficulty was a problem with reading. About nine out of ten of pupils with learning problems and about seven out of ten of all children with special educational needs were described as poor readers. Usually such children also had other learning problems.

Behaviour problems formed the next largest category of special educational needs. Children with behaviour difficulties often also had learning problems. Teachers were sensitive to a variety of behavioural and emotional difficulties and did not automatically describe a child who had behaviour problems as presenting discipline problems too: only about a half of the children with behaviour problems were thus described, and the possible difficulties of the withdrawn and unhappy child were not overlooked.

Although schools in the sample varied in the proportion of their pupils who were regarded as having special educational needs, it was not found that special needs were concentrated in a few 'problem' schools. All schools had pupils with special educational needs, and the schools with the highest proportions of such children contained, nevertheless, only a minority of the total of children with difficulties. This distribution of special needs corroborates the belief expressed in the Warnock Report that special educational needs should be of concern to all teachers and to the whole of the school system.

When the teachers in the sample described (as most of them did) pupils in their classes who had special educational needs, a greater variation appeared between the proportion of children identified by teachers than between the proportions located in different schools. The variation between teachers suggests that teachers are not applying a simple criterion and automatically describing five or six pupils in their classes without regard to the overall levels of difficulty. It also suggests (and this was confirmed in the interviews) that teacher responses were not influenced by knowledge of the contents of the Warnock Report. The variations between teachers will clearly reflect real differences between pupils in different classes. But they may also reflect differences in the views of individual teachers have of special needs and differences in the institutional contexts in which they work.

The largest category of learning difficulty described by teachers was that of 'poor reader'. As would be expected, there is a strong correspondence between this assessment made by a teacher and a child's performance on a reading test. Most of the children described as poor readers were at least a year behind their chronological age and a substantial minority were two years or more behind.

A comparison of reading scores, teacher assessments and other variables suggests that certain other characteristics of pupils and classrooms may influence teacher assessments. At particular levels of reading difficulty, boys were more likely than girls, children with behaviour problems were more likely than children without them, and younger children within a class were more likely than older children to be identified as poor readers. In addition, children in classes where the overall level of performance is high are more likely to be identified as poor readers than children with the same level of difficulty who are in classes where the overall standard is lower.

This suggests that assessments could sometimes be improved, and one of the areas investigated in the research was the use of formal assessment techniques. Teachers are continually making assessments of the children in their classes, and an element of this assessment is often a child's score on a standardised test. The use of tests is very widespread indeed. Reading tests in particular were used in over 90 per cent of the classrooms visited. Although a certain proportion of this testing formed part of the testing programme of the LEA, schools conducted testing on their own account also, and the majority of schools located in authorities which did not have a testing programme still used tests on their own initiative. It is decidedly not the case that testing is a practice imposed by LEAs on unwilling schools.

Both LEAs and schools most frequently test reading, but different tests are favoured. LEAs are inclined to use tests that involve reading for meaning, but schools show a distinct preference for word-recognition tests. This type of test is extremely limited in the amount of information which it gives about a child's reading skill and is particularly inappropriate for poor readers, as there is no diagnostic element.

The choice of tests would indicate that, on the whole, teachers' knowledge of testing is not very extensive, and this criticism applies, with a very limited number of exceptions, to remedial teachers also, in whom more familiarity with a variety of testing procedures would be very advantageous. Frequently, test scores were recorded in such a way that they could in fact mislead a teacher about a child's abilities. Improved recording procedures should be relatively easy to introduce.

Although there is a substantial literature on the significance of discrepancies between teachers' assessments and test scores in terms of who is right – teacher or test – this is a naive and unfruitful approach to the issue. Frequently, teacher assessment and test score are not independent of each other, as the test score is, in the context of classroom practice, often part of the teacher assessment. Even when the two are completely separate they are most profitably considered as two pieces of information about a child: any discrepancy between the two is of interest, but one is not necessarily more accurate, reliable or informative than the other.

When faced with discrepancies between their own opinions and pupils' test scores, teachers do tend to favour their own assessments, but very few are prepared simply to ignore the test results. Teachers are most likely to change their opinion of a child's abilities if his test score is higher than expected. They are, on the whole, prepared to give the child the benefit of the doubt and seriously to consider the possibility that he has talents that have not been recognised before.

The use of tests cannot provide a teacher with a complete and infallible account of a child's ability, but the proper use of appropriate tests can provide valuable information and give teachers extra insight into the strengths and weaknesses of their pupils. To use tests in this way, however, most teachers need expert assistance.

The value of accurate assessment is directly related to the purposes for which it is conducted and the consequences for pupils of being assessed in various ways. Assessment of children's difficulties is of value only if appropriate remedial steps follow. This investigation has shown that accurate assessment of special needs is at times hampered by the teacher's perception of certain types of pupil as being more or less likely than other types to have difficulties. Thus, if appropriate provision is available, undiagnosed children may be missing out on it, although if it is not available they may merely be avoiding the possible disadvantage of being labelled as slow.

It must be remembered that the situation described in relation to the type and level of provision in the LEAs and schools relates to the situation in 1982, before the implementation of the 1981 Education Act. Nevertheless, the Warnock Report had been published four years earlier in 1978, and the 1981 Act had been passed and draft circulars for its implementation issued. Although the Act may result in changes in provision there is every reason to believe that any changes made will be very heavily influenced by the previous situation. In fact, officers in the authorities claimed that although the preparation of statements was a major new responsibility introduced by the Act, in many other respects there would not be any sudden major changes, because policy in the authorities had been influenced by the climate of opinion that preceded the Warnock Report. Nevertheless, Warnock must be regarded as a major landmark which resulted in special education and allied issues coming to the attention of everyone concerned with education instead of being something of a backwater.

All the authorities visited had instigated a variety of programmes for the integration of 'handicapped' pupils into ordinary schools, and typically this was the central issue in relation to policy concerning special educational needs. It was clear that it was the 2 per cent of children who were placed in special schools and who were traditionally the concern of special education that were the focus of attention, rather than the nearer 20 per cent of children in ordinary schools whom Warnock considered to have special educational needs.

Although support services run by the LEAs, especially the school psychological service and the remedial services, do offer assistance to schools to help them to cope with at least some of the 20 per cent, nevertheless both assessment of and provision for the majority of children with special educational needs is, in large part, left to the individual schools. Both heads and class teachers are willing to cater for the vast majority of children but whether they are always able to do this adequately is another matter. During a period of more restricted expenditure on education many authorities had reduced the number of part-time teaching hours available in schools, and the majority of heads felt that this had indirectly made a serious impact on the provision schools could make for children with special educational needs.

The most frequent and the most popular type of provision in junior schools is extra help with learning, and especially with reading difficulties, through withdrawal from the regular classroom. A large number of children receive this help, and teachers would like it for many more, but despite this enthusiasm it appears that teachers do not think that children who are withdrawn are more likely to overcome their learning problems than children who do not get such assistance. It would appear that there is considerable willingness to accept as many children with special needs as possible into the regular school and to cope with them as well as possible. On the other hand, regular schools do need to have this willingness channelled into the right directions and given ample support.

The support that might usefully be given to teachers would include reassurance that a child's difficulties are not imported into the school as static and stubborn properties but are, more often than is believed, amenable to remedial influences within the school. Almost without exception, teachers view the difficulties of their pupils as arising from factors innate to the child or from elements in his home environment or from a combination of these. In the case of learning difficulties, innate factors are seen to predominate with home factors an important secondary influence. In the case of behaviour problems this pattern is reversed; home and related factors are seen to predominate but innate characteristics are also seen as important. It was unusual for a teacher to view a child's difficulties as arising from factors within the control of the teacher or the school.

The majority of teachers have had experience of a child in their class who they thought had difficulties so severe that the child could

151

be regarded as fitting into one of the old statutory categories of handicap. The most common experience was of ESN(M) children, followed by maladjusted children, but teachers had also had experience of pupils with physical handicaps and sensory impairments.

When the teachers were asked how they would feel about having children with various types of handicap in the ordinary classroom, it was clear that they had a warmer welcome for the idea of children with physical and sensory disabilities than they had for the idea of children with severe learning problems and behavioural problems. For any particular type of handicap, having had experience of a child with that disability in the classroom was associated with an increased willingness to have a child of that sort in the future. But, overall, it was at the prospect of the type of problem with which teachers were most familiar, those associated with learning and behaviour, that enthusiasm for integration was at its lowest.

Systematic observation of classrooms reveals an overall pattern of classroom activities and interactions similar to that which emerges from other observational studies of primary classrooms. The class-rooms in the study were quiet and orderly, and characterised by high levels of work and work-related activities. In particular, the children spend a good deal of time working on their own on curriculum tasks. This individualised pattern of work, typical of English primary schools, creates difficulties for the teacher in attempting to work with pupils on an individual basis while managing the classroom activities of a class of thirty children. This difficulty arises particularly in the case of children with special educational needs, who are particularly likely to require an individualised work programme and who may also pose problems of classroom management.

Children identified as having learning problems were found to have rather different patterns of behaviour from those of other pupils. In particular, they spend less time working on curriculum activities and more time distracted from them. This distracted activity is typically spent on their own rather than interacting with other pupils. Such pupils also have high levels of fidgeting. Children identified by their teachers as having reading problems but not as being all-round slow learners differ from this behaviour pattern and have patterns of activities more typical of children without learning problems.

All the pupils with special educational needs received higher levels of attention from the teacher than did other children in the class, but this necessarily amounted to only a small proportion of the time they

152

spent in school. This extra undivided attention is clearly not enough to increase their level of engagement in work to that achieved by most pupils. It was noticeable, however, that the children with special needs were more strongly influenced than other pupils by types of classroom organisation, in that their involvement in work varied according to the type of organisation more than was general. There is other evidence for the effects of this kind of 'behavioural ecology' (Wheldall et al., 1981), and teachers may find it useful to consider carefully patterns of classroom organisation which can reduce the difficulties some children present in class. Working in small groups with the teacher made a much greater difference to the involvement in curriculum tasks of children with special educational needs than it did for other pupils.

The Warnock Report recognised that to meet children's special educational needs adequately would require a major effort of in-service education of teachers. The necessity for this kind of in-service provision is explicitly recognised by the teachers and heads in this study and also arises implicitly from other aspects of the work. The results presented here show a basic orientation towards special educational needs which closely matches that of the Warnock Report and an explicit recognition of the responsibilities of schools and teachers in this area. They also show the necessity for teachers to work together and with expert assistance to solve the classroom management problems that such children present, to improve on assessment procedures and, most of all, to develop an orientation towards overcoming, as well as recognising, the special difficulties of one in five of their pupils.

Appendix   Research design, sampling and analysis

The research aims to describe special educational needs in junior schools as seen by class teachers and then to describe various features of pupils, classrooms, schools and local support services relevant to special educational needs and to teachers' perceptions of them. This involves gathering a variety of different types of data from a variety of different sources. The major sorts of information required include:

Information from teachers about pupils in their classes with special educational needs.

Background data from these teachers including details of assessment procedures and their use of services relevant to special needs.

Information from head teachers about school procedures for dealing with special needs.

Information from remedial teachers about remedial procedures in the school.

Test data on children's achievements.

Observation of children's classroom behaviour.

Details of the organisation of support services in different local authorities.

The different types of data required raise complex problems of research design and sampling. They will be presented below as two interconnected studies; a survey of special educational needs in the junior school and a classroom-focused study of children with special educational needs. It should be explained that the research has always been conceptualised as a whole and that some of the questions which are addressed in the various chapters relate to data drawn from more than one aspect of the work.

A survey of special educational needs

The fundamental purpose of the survey was to describe the special educational needs of junior-age children as seen by their teachers. Important considerations in the research design were: to obtain information from a large and representative sample of teachers, to use data collection methods which would accurately reflect teachers' own views and to obtain a very high response rate from the sample.

An initial decision in educational research of this kind is whether sampling procedures should focus on individuals or on institutions such as schools. In some ways the educational system is organised conveniently for research purposes, in that the co-operation of a small number of schools, once it is secured, provides the researcher with a large number of teachers and children. Such a procedure, however, has its dangers as it introduces a strong clustering effect into the research design. In such a situation teachers and pupils have not been sampled independently of other pupils and teachers in the study, and factors which influence the variables may be common to them even though they are unusual in the educational system as a whole. A sample of a thousand children in one school is not generalisable to children in the whole country in the way that a random sample across the country would be. Nevertheless, the issue is not simply one of balancing the convenience of sampling institutions against the statistical efficiency of sampling individuals. Factors connected with the institutional location of the individuals studied are not just potentially contaminating influences on the results but may be important explanatory variables which should themselves also be studied. For example, a child's achievements should be considered in the context of classroom experience, and this may also involve studying his teacher and classmates. A teacher's view of special educational needs is best considered in the context of school arrangements for dealing with them, the availability of local support services and, perhaps, the views of his headteacher and colleagues.

When this approach is followed, there are considerable analytical as well as practical advantages in sampling institutions and then studying all or most of the individuals within them. Within this strategy of sampling institutions, the emphasis of the research was on representing the experience of individuals, and the sampling strategy therefore drew on institutions in proportion to the number of individuals within them; it was not the intention that sampling should be

155

representative of the institutions themselves. This meant that types of local education authority were stratified in proportion to the number of people they contained rather than according to the numbers of authorities of different types, and schools were stratified by size so as not to over-represent teachers and pupils in small schools.

Sampling

Ten local education authorities were sampled at random within a stratification system designed to produce six county authorities, three metropolitan authorities and one London borough. Exceptions to this random procedure were that three authorities with extensive middle-school systems were excluded because of the difficulty of comparing them with primary schools, and the sampling ensured that at least one authority fairly convenient for the location of the research team would be included in view of the classroom-focused stage of the research. As can be seen in Table A.1, this sampling pattern was designed to represent the experience of individuals rather than to represent types of authority. For example, county or non-metropolitan authorities make up 40.6 per cent of authorities but contain 60.5 per cent of pupils. Consequently six of the ten sample authorities were of this type. Of the ten authorities originally sampled nine agreed to take part. The tenth authority was replaced by an LEA of the same type.

Table A.1 Sample of local authorities

Local education authorities	Sample	DES statistics 1979	
		N of authorities	% of pupils
London Boroughs	1	21 (21.9%)	13.0%
Metropolitan Districts	3	36 (37.5%)	26.6%
Non-Metropolitan Authorities (not including Scilly Isles)	6	39 (40.6%)	60.5%

In eight of the sample LEAs, five junior or primary schools were randomly sampled within a stratification system controlling for size of school. This was to avoid the under-representation of pupils in large schools discussed above. In the other two LEAs ten schools were sampled using the same procedure. The difference in numbers of schools was because of the requirements of the classroom-focused study. In addition, in one authority, an extra school was included in

Table A.2 Sample of schools

Schools	Sample		DES statistics 1979 (junior and junior with infant)	
N of pupils	N	%	% of schools	% of pupils
0– 50	2	3.3	8.2	1.4
51–100	3	4.9	12.7	4.7
101–200	14	23.0	32.3	24.7
201–300	27	44.3	28.9	35.3
301–400	10	16.4	12.2	20.7
401 +	5	8.2	5.7	13.2
Total	61	100.0	100.0	100.0

order to represent a particular type of provision, that of a special unit within an ordinary school. Of the sixty-one schools originally sampled, fifty-nine or 96.7 per cent agreed to take part in the study. Both of the other two schools were replaced. This sampling procedure resulted in sixty-one schools ranging in size from below fifty children to over 400. All schools were either junior (7–11) or primary (5–11), although only the junior age range was of concern in this study. The figures in Table A.2 show that in comparison with the DES figures the project over-represents larger schools, although the match between the numbers of pupils in schools of different sizes in the sample and in the DES statistics is still not exact. There is a tendency for the sample to over-represent pupils in small and medium-size schools and to under-represent those in the largest schools.

In these schools there were a total of 440 junior classes; 428 class teachers, representing 97.3 per cent of the classes in the study, were interviewed. No teacher refused to take part. Non-response occurred only in cases where, despite visits to a school at various points in the year, it was impossible to interview a teacher who had taken the class for at least half a term, which was considered to be a minimum period in view of the types of question being asked.

Some basic demographic characteristics of the teachers in the sample as compared with DES statistics are shown in Table A.3. The ratio of men to women in the sample is almost identical to that in junior schools nationally; in both sets of figures seven out of ten of the teachers are female. The age distribution of the sample is also close to the national figures, with some tendency for the sample teachers to be

Table A.3 Demographic characteristics of sample teachers

Teachers	Sample		DES statistics 1979	
			Junior and junior with infants	Junior only
	N	%	%	%
Sex: Male	125	29.2	23.4	30.6
Female	303	70.8	76.6	69.4
			Primary (including nursery and primary deemed middle) %	
Age: < 25	28	6.5	9.0	
25–29	88	20.6	21.2	
30–34	92	21.5	14.8	
35–39	54	12.6	12.0	
40–44	55	12.9	13.2	
45 +	111	25.9	29.8	
Total:	428	100.0		

closer to the middle age range than nationally. Just over a quarter of the sample teachers were under thirty and about the same proportion are forty-five or over. Both equivalent national figures are close to 30 per cent.

In addition to the class teachers, the sixty-one head teachers were also interviewed, as were thirty-seven remedial teachers in the schools. Particular emphasis was given to the importance of obtaining high response rates, and this is reflected in the overall level of response. The response rate among LEAs was 90 per cent, among schools 96.7 per cent and among teachers (or classes) 97.3 per cent. However, no teacher refused to take part; the non-response was a result of classes not having a permanent teacher at the times the research team visited the school. Clearly these classes could not be replaced in the sample but the non-responding LEA and the two non-responding schools were replaced.

Data collection

It was decided that the primary method of data collection for the survey should be personal interviews with teachers and heads conducted by members of the research team. Although this is a relatively time-consuming method of data gathering, compared, for example, with a postal questionnaire, the kind of information required and the necessity to maximise response rates made it essential.

Following initial contacts with schools, one or more members of the research team arranged to visit a school, usually for several days. Teachers were introduced to the research project either at a staff meeting or individually, and each class teacher was asked to make a note of children in their class whom they considered to have special educational needs. At this stage no further definition was offered. Individual interviews with each teacher followed, usually lasting about an hour. For each child identified by a teacher a note was made of the teacher's description of the child's special needs. The research then went through the set of descriptions generated in the pilot study (Moses, 1982) and asked of each child: is the child a slow learner, a poor reader, does he or she have a behaviour problem, have a physical handicap, have hearing or sight impairments, have other health problems, present a discipline problem or have any other special educational needs? The descriptions initially given by the teachers almost always fell into one of these categories, although the additional categories of speech problems and English as a second language were generated by the teacher responses. Having described the children initially nominated in terms of these categories, the teachers were asked if there were any further children they wished to describe. In fact over 90 per cent of the pupils described by teachers were initially identified without this prompting, and most of the types of difficulty described were part of the teacher's original description of a child rather than in response to specific prompts. After describing a pupil's difficulties the teacher was then asked about any special provision being made for the child or that the teacher would like to see being made, about any special help or advice she had received concerning the child, about the causes of the child's difficulties and about the extent to which she thought they would be overcome.

After the discussion of individual children the teachers were then interviewed about their testing and record-keeping procedures, their contact with specialist services relevant to special educational needs, in particular the school psychological service, and their experience of and attitudes towards the integration of handicapped children into the ordinary classroom. Wherever reading ages from tests administered within the school were available, as was usually the case, these were obtained. Interviews were also conducted with the head teacher focusing on the school's procedures for identifying and dealing with special educational needs, school practice on testing and record-keeping, relationships with specialist agencies relevant to special educational needs and the head's own experience of and attitudes towards the integration of handicapped pupils in ordinary schools. Copies of school record forms and any other relevant materials were also gathered.

Finally, interviews were conducted with any remedial teachers in the school about the arrangements for remedial work, the way children were identified as needing special help and the kind of help they received. Details of the remedial teacher's view of the nature of the difficulties of each of the pupils whom she saw were also obtained except where one teacher saw a very large number of pupils, and here a sample was taken. All interviews were carried out by one of the three members of the research team and were conducted in private in the school. This survey was carried out principally during the spring and summer terms of 1981. The sample and data are summarised in Table A.4.

Table A.4 Survey of special educational needs in junior classrooms

Sample	Data
428 junior class teachers, 61 head teachers and 37 remedial teachers in 61 junior/primary schools randomly sampled in 10 LEAs.	Interviews with junior class teachers including descriptions of pupils in their classes with special educational needs. Interviews with head teachers. Interviews with remedial teachers including descriptions of pupils getting remedial help. Pupil's reading ages, where available, from school records. Copies of school record-keeping procedures.

Classroom-focused study

The second major aspect of the research was an attempt to study in more detail the performance and behaviour of pupils identified by their teachers as having special educational needs and to compare these with the performance and behaviour of their classmates. In this way it was intended to relate characteristics of the children, derived independently of their teachers' assessments, to the children's special needs and to the teachers' perceptions of them as having special needs. This information was obtained from two testing procedures, a reading test and a non-verbal reasoning test, and from systematic observation of children with special educational needs and control children in the classroom.

Systematic observation is a technique which enables different observers to describe pupil and teacher behaviour using identical classification procedures and therefore allows comparable descriptions of different individuals and different classrooms. (See Galton, Simon and Croll, 1980, for an example of the use of this technique.) It is an extremely demanding procedure in that a large number of observations are required in order to build up a reliable description of individuals and classes, and this necessitates lengthy periods of observation. In consequence it was not practicable to carry out this research on the same scale as the survey.

The detailed classroom-focused study was carried out in thirty-four second-year classes in two of the local authorities from the original sample: these classes were chosen for their relative convenience for the research team and as representing different types of authorities. These authorities were the two in which ten schools originally had been sampled, and the thirty-four classes represented all but one of the second-year classes in these twenty schools. This stage of the research was carried out during the second year of the study, in the autumn term of 1981 and the spring and summer terms of 1982. The pupils in these classes had been first-year juniors, generally with different teachers, when the survey was carried out, so that a longitudinal element in looking at the assessments made by different teachers of the same children was also possible. Most of the teachers had been interviewed during the previous school year as part of the survey.

The number of classes involved was determined by the time-consuming nature of observational research and the level of resources available. Within these constraints it was decided to concentrate on a single age group in order to avoid the additional complication of different year groups in the analysis. First years were excluded to avoid effects related to differences between all-through primary schools and separate junior schools and also possible differences in the rate at which children 'settle in' to a school. Fourth years were excluded in order to avoid influences on assessments from different sorts of secondary schools to which the children would transfer. The choice of second years from the remaining two groups was arbitrary. In these thirty-four classes teachers were initially asked to describe pupils having special educational needs in the same way as had been done in the survey. They were also asked to complete the Rutter Child Behaviour Questionnaire for the class (Rutter, 1967). The researchers then administered the SPAR reading test (Young, 1981) and an NFER non-verbal reasoning test (Pidgeon, 1970). Pupils were selected for observation on the basis of the teachers' descriptions and the test results, being regarded as candidates for observation if their teacher described them as slow learners or poor readers or as having behaviour problems or constituting a discipline problem, but not if their only problems were connected with health or with a sensory impairment or physical handicap. Pupils were also eligible to be observed if their teachers were surprised at their test results. (The results had been discussed with the teacher.) In addition, pupils whose reading-test scores were below the median score for pupils described by their teacher as poor readers but had not themselves been so described were included in the observation. Up to six pupils with special educational needs or with surprising test results were observed in each class along with four control children, two boys and two girls chosen at random from the remaining pupils. Consequently between four and ten pupils could be observed in each class. The average number of children observed was over eight per class. The teachers did not know which children or how many children were being observed but did know that at least some of the children they discussed with the researchers would be selected. Results from the analysis of the observation data discussed in the report suggest that this did not influence the level of teacher interactions with their pupils. In addition to individual pupils, the teacher herself was also observed directly in order to provide more detail of teacher contacts with the selected pupils and to help provide an overall view of the classroom.

The systematic observation procedure was based on that of Moses (1982). Two observation schedules were used, one for the teacher and one for pupils. A time-sampling system under which behaviour was coded at ten-second intervals was used. Observation focused on one pupil at a time for four minutes or twenty-four codes. The pupil's behaviour was coded in terms of his activity (working, distracted, etc.), his interaction with other pupils and the teacher and whether or not he was fidgeting or moving around the classroom. In addition, the nature of the class activity (a class lesson, individual work, etc.) and of

Table A.5 Classroom-focused study of pupils with special educational needs

Sample	Data
34 2nd-year classes in 20 schools. Test data on 762 pupils. Observational data on 280 pupils (151 pupils with special needs, 129 controls).	Teacher descriptions of pupils with special needs. Teacher assessments of pupils on Rutter child behaviour questionnaire. Reading-test scores (SPAR). Non-verbal reasoning test (NFER). Systematic observation of classroom behaviour and interactions: 720 observations of each child spread over a total of 2 hours (but not consecutive for 2 hours); 1800 observations of each teacher spread over a total of 5 hours (but not consecutive for 5 hours).

the child's curriculum activity (reading, maths, etc.) was coded whenever the activity changed. Observation focused on the teacher also recorded behaviour at ten-second intervals. The teachers' classroom activities were coded in terms of their content and the focus of their interaction. In particular, interactions with any of the pupils who were under observation were noted and the pupils were identified. Teachers' interactions were coded for positive and negative content and tone whenever this was applicable.

All the time in school that the class spent with their teacher was included in the observation, not only lesson time. Each pupil observed was coded on 720 occasions, covering a total of two hours. Each teacher observed was coded on a total of 1800 observations over a total of five hours. These observations were spread throughout the hours (up to twenty-five) of observation time spent in each classroom.

For thirty-four second-year classes these procedures provide test data on all the pupils in the class and observation data on all the teachers and a sample of the pupils. This makes it possible to look at the behaviour and performance of pupils identified as having special educational needs in the context in which they occur and at possible influences of these factors on teacher assessments.

Bibliography

AINSCOW, M. and TWEDDLE, D. (1979), *Preventing Classroom Failure: An Objectives Approach*, Chichester, Wiley.

ARNOLD, H. (1977), 'The Teacher's Perception of the Pupil's Reading Ability' in Gilliland, J. (ed.), *Reading: Research and Clasroom Practice*, London, Ward Lock.

ASHTON, P., KNEEN, P., DAVIES, F. and HOLLEY, B. J. (1975), *The Aims of Primary Education: a Study of Teachers' Opinions*, London, Macmillan Education.

ASPIN, D. N. (1982), 'Towards a Concept of Human Being as a Basis for a Philosophy of Special Education', *Educational Review*, vol. 34, no. 2.

BASSEY, M. (1981), '131 Primary School Teachers' Opinions about their College Training', *Education Researchal*, vol. 22, no. 3.

BENNETT, N. (1976), *Teaching Styles and Pupil Progress*, London, Open Books.

BOYDELL, D. (1978), *The Primary Teacher in Action*, London, Open Books.

BROOKS, V. (1983), 'An Evaluation of the S.N.A.P. Programme', University of Leicester (mimeo).

BROPHY, J. (1979), 'Teacher Behaviour and its Effects', *Journal of Educational Psychology*, vol. 71, no. 6.

BURT, C. (1921), *Mental and Scholastic Tests*, London, King & Son.

BURT, C. (1944), *The Young Delinquent*, London, University of London Press.

BURT, C. (1952), *The Causes and Treatment of Backwardness*, London, National Children's Home.

CHAZAN, M., LAING, A. F., SHACKLETON BAILEY, M. and JONES, G. (1980), *Some of our Children*, London, Open Books.

COARD, B. (1971), *How the West Indian Child is Made Educationally Subnormal in the English School System*, London, New Beacon Books.

CROLL, P. (1981), 'Social Class, Pupil Achievement and Classroom Interaction' in Simon, B. and Willcocks, J. (eds), *Research and Practice in the Primary Classroom*, London, Routledge & Kegan Paul.

DEPARTMENT OF EDUCATION AND SCIENCE (1967), *Children and their Primary Schools* (The Plowden Report), London, Her Majesty's Stationery Office.

DEPARTMENT OF EDUCATION AND SCIENCE (1975), *A Language for Life* (The Bullock Report), London, Her Majesty's Stationery Office.

DEPARTMENT OF EDUCATION AND SCIENCE (1978), *Special Educational Needs* (The Warnock Report), London, Her Majesty's Stationery Office.

DEPARTMENT OF EDUCATION AND SCIENCE (1983), *Report by H.M.I. on the Effects of the Local Authority Expenditure Policies on the Education Service in England 1981*, Department of Education and Science.

DOUGLAS, J.W.B. (1967), *The Home and the School*, St Albans, Panther.

DRIVER, C. (1980), 'How West Indian Pupils Do Better at School', *New Society*, 17.1.80.

FLOUD, J. and HALSEY, A. H. (1957), 'Intelligence Tests, Social Class and Selection for Secondary Schools', *British Journal of Sociology*, vol. 8, no. 1.

GALTON, M., SIMON, B., and CROLL, P. (1980), *Inside the Primary Classroom*, London, Routledge & Kegan Paul.

GALTON, M. and CROLL, P. (1980), 'Pupil Progress in Basic Skills' in Galton, M. and Simon, B. (eds), *Progress and Performance in the Primary Classroom*, London, Routledge & Kegan Paul.

GIPPS, C. and WOOD, R. (1981), 'The Testing of Reading in LEAs: The Bullock Report Seven Years On', *Educational Studies*, vol. 7, no. 3.

HALSEY, A.H. and GARDINER, L. (1953), 'Selection for Secondary Education and Achievement in Four Grammar Schools', *British Journal of Sociology*, vol. 4.

HEGARTY, S. and POCKLINGTON, K. (1981a), *Educating Pupils with Special Needs in the Ordinary School*, Windsor, NFER-Nelson.

HEGARTY, S. and POCKLINGTON, K. (1981b), *Integration in Action*, Windsor, NFER-Nelson.

HERBERT, M. (1975), *Problems of Childhood*, London, Pan.

KASH, M.M. and MOORE, J.M. (1982), 'Pupil Characteristics, Pupil Behaviours and their Relationships to Pupil Performance', *Aspects of Education*, 27.

MARSHALL, C. and WOLFENDALE, S. (1977), 'Screening and Early Identification of Children with Problems' in Gilliland, J. (ed.), *Reading: Research and Classroom Practice*, London, Ward Lock.

MERRETT, F. and WHELDALL, K. (1978), 'Playing the Game: a Behavioural Approach to Classroom Management in the Junior School', *Educational Review*, vol. 30, no. 1.

MOSES, D. (1980), 'The Assessment and Incidence of Special Educational Needs', University of Leicester (mimeo).

MOSES, D. (1982), 'Special Educational Needs: the Relationship between Teacher Assessment, Test Scores and Classroom Behaviour', *British Educational Research Journal*, vol. 8, no. 2.

PIDGEON, D. (1970), *Test 28 Non-verbal Test BD,* Windsor, NFER.

PRESLAND, J. (1976), 'Modifying Behaviour NOW', *Special Education Forward Trends*, vol. 3.

PRINGLE, M.L.K., BUTLER, N.R. and DAVIE, R. (1966), *Eleven Thousand Seven-Year-Olds* (First report of the National Child Development Study), London, Longman.

165

BIBLIOGRAPHY

PUMPHREY, P.D. (1977), *Measuring Reading Abilities: Concepts, Sources and Applications*, London, Hodder & Stoughton.

RUTTER, M. (1967), 'A Children's Behaviour Questionnaire for Completion by Teachers', *Journal of Child Psychology and Psychiatry*, vol. 8, pp. 1–11.

RUTTER, M., TIZARD, J. and WHITMORE, K. (1970), *Education, Health and Behaviour*, London, Longman.

RUTTER, M., MAUGHAN, B., MORTIMORE, P. and OUSTON, J. (1979), *Fifteen Thousand Hours: Secondary Schools and their Effects on Children*, London, Open Books.

SALMON-COX, L. (1981), 'Teachers and Standardised Achievement Tests: What's Really Happening?', *Phi Delta Kappa*, May 1981.

SATTERLY, D. (1981), *Assessment in Schools*, Oxford, Basil Blackwell.

SCHONELL, F.J. (1961), *The Psychology and Teaching of Reading*, London, Oliver & Boyd.

SOUTHGATE, V., ARNOLD, H. and JOHNSON, S. (1981), *Extending Beginning Reading*, London, Heinemann/Schools Council.

SQUIBB, P. (1981), 'A Theoretical Structuralist Approach to Special Education' in Barton, L. and Tomlinson, S. (eds), *Special Education: Policy, Practices and Social Issues*, London, Harper & Row.

STOTT, D.H. (1982), 'Behaviour Disturbance and Failure to Learn', *Aspects of Education*, vol. 27.

TANSLEY, P. and PANKHURST, J. (1981), *Children with Specific Learning Difficulties*, Windsor, NFER-Nelson.

TAYLOR, M. (1982), *Caught Between*, Windsor, NFER-Nelson.

TOMLINSON, S. (1981), *Educational Subnormality – A Study in Decision Making*, London, Routledge & Kegan Paul.

TOWNSEND, P. and DAVIDSON, N. (1982), *Inequalities in Health*, Harmondsworth, Penguin.

WHELDALL, K., MORRIS, M., VAUGHAN P. and YIN YUK NG (1981), 'Rows versus Tables: an Example of the Use of Behavioural Ecology in Two Classes of Eleven-year-old Children', *Educational Psychology*, vol. 1, no. 2, pp. 171–84.

WILLIAMS, H., MUNCEY, J. and WINTERINGHAM, D. (1980), *Precision Teaching: A Classroom Manual*, Coventry School Psychological Service.

YOUNG, D. (1981), *The Spelling and Reading Test*, London, Hodder & Stoughton.

YOUNGMAN, M.D. (1982), 'Behaviour as an Indicator of Pupils' Academic Performance', *Aspects of Education*, 27.

Index

Ainscow, M., 44, 164
Arnold, H., 68, 164, 166
Ashton, P., 124, 164
Aspin, D. N., 11, 12, 164

Barton, L., 166
Bassey, M., 6, 164
Bennett, S. N., 43, 164
Boydell, D., 68, 164
Brooks, V., 7, 102, 164
Brophy, J., 44, 164
Bullock, A., 78, 80, 82
Burt, C., 42, 80, 81, 82, 83
Butler, N. R., 3, 165

Chazan, M., 58, 164
Coard, B., 33, 164
Croll, P., 44, 68, 85, 104, 121, 123, 127, 161, 164, 165

Davidson, N., 37, 166
Davie, R., 3, 165
Davies, F., 164
Douglas, J. W. B., 67, 165
Driver, C., 33, 165

Floud, J., 43, 165

Galton, M., 43, 85, 104, 121, 123, 127, 161, 165
Gardiner, L., 43, 165
Gilliland, J., 164, 165
Gipps, C., 79, 82, 165

Halsey, A. H., 43, 165
Hegarty, S., 2, 51, 56, 165
Herbert, M., 28, 165
Holley, B. J., 164

Johnson, S., 166
Jones, G., 164

Kash, M. M., 70, 165
Kneen, P., 164

Laing, A. F., 164

Marshall, C., 15, 165
Maughan, B., 166
Merrett, F., 44, 165
Moore, J. M., 70, 165
Morris, M., 166
Mortimore, P., 166
Moses, D., 25, 27, 57, 69, 74, 126, 128, 133, 137, 144, 159, 162, 165
Muncey, J., 44, 166

National Children's Bureau, 3, 18, 43, 67, 70, 165
National Foundation for Educational Research, 2, 50, 56

Ouston, J., 166

Panckhurst, J., 24, 25, 166
Pidgeon, D., 162, 165
Plowden, B., 43, 48, 67, 121, 164
Pocklington, K., 2, 51, 56, 165
Presland, J., 44, 165
Pringle, M. L. K., 3, 18, 31, 37, 43, 70, 165
Pumphrey, P. D., 84, 166

Rutter, M., 3, 13, 16, 24, 31, 44, 70, 162, 166

INDEX

Salmon-Cox, L., 91, 166
Satterley, D., 15, 166
Schonell, F. J., 80, 81, 82, 83, 166
Schools Council, 124
Shackleton Bailey, M., 164
Simon, B., 104, 121, 123, 127, 161, 164, 165
Squibb, P., 18, 166
Stott, D. H., 70, 166

Tansley, P., 24, 25, 166
Taylor, M., 33, 166
Tizard, J., 3, 31, 70, 166
Tomlinson, S., 18, 33, 166
Townsend, P., 37, 166
Tweddle, D., 44, 164

Vaughan, P., 166

Warnock, M., 1, 2, 4, 5, 6, 8, 9, 12, 13, 20, 24, 34, 37, 40, 41, 50, 76, 92, 96, 97, 99, 102, 147, 148, 150, 153, 165
Wheldall, K., 44, 153, 165, 166
Whitmore, K., 3, 31, 70, 166
Willcocks, J., 164
Williams, H., 44, 166
Winteringham, D., 44, 166
Wolfendale, S., 15, 165
Wood, R., 79, 82, 165

Yin Yuk Ng, 166
Young, D., 79, 82, 162, 166
Youngman, M. D., 70, 166